HMO PROPER_ _

RENOVATION &

REFURBISHMENT

SUCCESS

TAKING YOUR BRICKS AND MORTAR FROM PURCHASE TO READY TO RENT

by Nick Fox & Richard Leonard

ISBN: 978-0-9927817-6-7

First published in England in 2015 by Fox Print Partners
Edited by Sarah Walker

HMO PROPERTY RENOVATION & REFURBISHMENT SUCCESS

TAKING YOUR BRICKS AND MORTAR FROM PURCHASE TO READY TO RENT

by Nick Fox & Richard Leonard

published by Fox Print Partners

Contents

For my family, friends and business partners.
You all inspire me daily.
Thank you.
Nick

To my family, but especially my son William, who has inspired me through his great courage and strength to take the step to make property my full-time occupation.
Thank you, Wills.
Richard x

About the authors

A prolific and highly successful investor, Nick Fox has been involved with property since his early childhood. Today, his investment portfolio includes more than 200 buy to let properties – both shared accommodation and single household lets – and he has interests in a number of development projects.

As is the case with so many successful businesspeople, Nick started young. When he was eight, he bought up all the penny sweets from the Scout Camp tuck shop and sold them on to his friends for 2p! His delight at doubling his money on his first business venture signposted an entrepreneurial attitude and launched an enthusiasm for making money on his own terms that has never left him.

His introduction to the property market came not long afterwards, when the caravan that he lived in with his mother burned down. She used the insurance money to buy a wreck of a house, which she did up and sold for a profit, repeating the process until they had a nice home. When he wasn't in school, Nick helped his mother out and began to understand not only what could be achieved by hard work, but also the potential of property as a money-making vehicle. He just needed a bit of capital to get him started.

In 1988, at the age of 19, Nick landed a job with a company that imported computer software from America and sold it into retailers in the UK. It didn't take long for Nick to see the technology boom that was starting and he quickly realised he could do the same thing himself.

Operating out of his bedroom, Nick took out as many credit cards as he could and bought software stock from all over the world. He started off selling into small retailers, then, when the market for personal computers really took off, he moved into proper premises and grew the company until it became the UK's leading budget software company, selling over a million units every month into Dixons, Woolworths and WHSmith.

But by 2002 business had peaked. Technology had gone mainstream and was even available in supermarkets, and things quickly declined for Nick.

2005 was the 'light bulb' moment, when he realised that the income from his various businesses might have paid for his lifestyle, but it was his home that had built equity and given him a lump-sum return. He knew that the quickest and only way he could replace his financial losses was to buy more properties.

By the end of 2005, Nick had five properties, all rented to friends, generating an income and building equity. He started buying larger homes, which he rented as single units to families, and by the end of the following year, Nick had 20 properties and a significant buy to let business.

In 2007, he went into a buying frenzy. Within 12 months, he'd added another 90 properties to his portfolio. Then, as the credit crunch hit and many of his mortgages moved off initial low fixed rates and onto variables, Nick started to look at how he could increase his profits and turned one of his existing family home lets into an HMO. That was light bulb moment number two.

He began to partner with other investors and subsequently doubled the size of his portfolio to more than 200 properties, around 100 of them HMOs. That portfolio is currently managed through the Milton Keynes letting agency he set up in 2010 and achieves 98% occupancy.

"Everyone thinks I must be constantly working to keep so many plates spinning but, really, I just employ great managers and develop effective systems."

Nick's HMO investment strategy is now highly regarded within the industry and he is regularly asked to speak at property investment events. His expertise is called on by new clients and fellow professional investors alike and his reputation has enabled him to establish a significant mentoring business.

Over the past few years, Nick has also acquired business interests outside property: a photography company that he's looking to franchise and investment in a local pre-school that serves 80 children and has been rated 'outstanding' by OFSTED.

Nick loves football, tennis, golf and boating and has climbed Mount Snowdon with his partner, Samantha. He is committed to supporting local charitable causes and is also a Patron of Peace One Day. He and Samantha live just outside St Albans with their five children.

Richard Leonard is a former technology project consultant with more than 20 years' experience in letting and managing property. Now a professional investor and project manager, he has a high income-generating personal portfolio worth over £3m and specialises in sourcing and refurbishing HMOs for clients in Hertfordshire.

At the ripe old age of 12, Richard set up his first business venture, cleaning cars at the weekend for 50p each. He soon realised he was on to a winner when he had to recruit three of his friends to work with him to satisfy demand. "I can still remember how pleased and proud I was to have my old tobacco tin heaving with coins by the end of every Sunday afternoon. It was certainly a good business model: low overheads, great profits and loyal customers!"

After studying Electronics at Cambridge, Richard entered the corporate world and by the early 1990s was designing and managing infrastructure and I.T. projects for a number of global finance and technology companies. By the end of the '90s he had built a technology consultancy, which he continued to grow and manage through the '00s, delivering complex and demanding solutions to a number of large corporate clients, including Catlin, Eversheds, Barclays and Coca-Cola.

At the same time, he was investing in property. His great-grandfather used to work as a handyman for a local landlord and Richard remembered it striking him, even when he was a young lad, as rather romantic that this old man was keeping people's homes safe and sound. "I think it gave me a subconscious love of property and fascination for property management, and then when I read 'The Richest Man in Babylon' and 'Rich Dad, Poor Dad' in my early twenties, I realised investment was the way forward and that using property as a vehicle was the most naturally comfortable fit."

He teamed up with a business partner based in Luton and they began to buy property at auction, snapping up absolute wrecks for peanuts and doing them up. Buy to let mortgages hadn't yet been introduced, so they simply used Richard's capital and took out as many credit cards as they could, then let the properties out to recover their investment.

That was all at a time when the private rented sector barely existed. As there were hardly any letting agents in the market, Richard and his partner decided early on that they should establish their own agency, through which they could market and let their own properties and also satisfy a growing local demand for letting and management services.

Within two years, they had a portfolio of 300 properties and the business had got too big for Richard, who was still working his 'day job' as a technology consultant! In their third year, he asked his partner to buy him out.

A decade on, keen for another property business opportunity, Richard started up a letting and maintenance company, covering Luton and the Home Counties. This allowed him to once again indulge his passion for property on a part-time basis, as he continued his career with the blue-chips, but a few years later his world was turned on its head.

At the age of six, Richard's son, William, was diagnosed with a brain tumour. Treatment in London was unsuccessful, so the family was forced to temporarily relocate to Oklahoma, where specialised procedures would give William the very best chance of survival and Richard knew he could no longer commit to the corporate world. His accountant advised him that his portfolio was providing a good income and suggested he focused more on that. When William piped up from his hospital bed, "Dad, you should do the properties again", the future was sealed.

And so, in 2014, having already met Nick and several other professional investors, Richard founded Stevenage Lettings. The company lets and manages both Richard's personal portfolio and properties for other local landlords and clients. His HMOs give him a gross annual income in excess of £100k, with each property achieving a return on investment of between 12% and 16% - a return he consistently achieves for his clients.

"One of my main reasons for investing in property was so that I could establish a passive income stream that would pay for my day-to-day expenditure. I didn't expect to achieve that so quickly – HMOs have proved quite a revelation for me!"

With so many years of experience under his belt, Richard now has a specific template for sourcing, renovating and refurbishing properties, with a refined system and a trusted team in place to deliver it.

Richard lives in Walkern, Hertfordshire, with his family. He's passionate about his motorcycling and is an avid Chelsea supporter.

Authors' disclaimer

We are not qualified to give financial or legal advice. All related recommendations made in this book should only be considered in consultation with suitably qualified and accredited professionals. Persons giving financial advice MUST be properly qualified and regulated by the Financial Services Authority (FSA) and anyone giving you legal advice should be suitably qualified and regulated by The Law Society and the Solicitors Regulation Authority (SRA) (or the Council of Licensed Conveyancers (CLC)).

Also by Nick Fox:

HMO Property Success

The Secrets of Buy to Let Success

Property Investment Success

Available in paperback from nickfox.co.uk & Amazon.co.uk.
Audiobook available from Amazon.co.uk, Audible.co.uk & iTunes.
Kindle and iBook formats also available.

Introduction

People renovate and refurbish properties for two reasons: because it's necessary and/or because they want to 'force' an increase in the value of their investment. That may be their own home or a property they want to improve and sell on immediately afterwards, but in a large number of cases – and certainly if it's an investment – most people are making improvements because they want to let the property.

As you'll be all too well aware if you've read the other books in the 'Success' series, buy to let investing is a business and, needless to say, a property is only worth buying if it makes good financial sense. And the renovation and refurbishment is where too many people make mistakes, either because they haven't prepared well enough and budgeted correctly, which means their initial capital investment is far greater than they anticipated, or because they simply don't carry out the work properly. That leads to greater on-going maintenance bills and more complaints from tenants, which often results in a higher tenant turnover and not being able to achieve the expected level of rent.

Long story short, if you don't get this stage of your property project right, your whole investment plan can come unstuck.

How you renovate and refurbish will vary, depending on what you intend to do with the property. You need to be clear on your target tenant market and what they expect from their home, then make sure that's what you provide. And this isn't a process you can simply get right once and then endlessly repeat; demands and standards change as time goes on, so you must keep up to date with the market and constantly tweak, refine and update your methods.

For the purposes of this book, we'll primarily look at the process of completely renovating and refurbishing a property for letting as a House in Multiple Occupation (HMO). Needless to say, if you're preparing a property for letting as a single unit, not everything will apply to you - although most will, and it's worth getting an idea of what's involved in preparing a multi-let, in case you choose to go down that route at a later date.

Preparation, Preparation, Preparation.
You can never do enough.

PART ONE:
PLANNING, BUDGETING AND PREPARING

"Before anything else, preparation is the key to success."

Alexander Graham Bell

Chapter 1

Preparing yourself

Property is very different to most other kinds of investment because it demands a lot more from you, in terms of time, effort and knowledge. At one end of the property investing scale is the 'hands-off' investment, but even then you need to carefully research the investment provider, the investment itself and your finance options. At the other end of the scale is the entirely 'hands-on' investment – the buy to let property that needs a thorough overhaul - and that's what we're talking about here.

Each element of property investment is a small business in itself, so treat the renovation and refurbishment part as you would any other business. You need to think about what lies ahead and whether you're willing, able and prepared to take everything on. In most cases, when things go wrong, it's because people don't have the right mindset, so preparing yourself, mentally, for the project really is key. Here are the most important things to consider:

Do you know what you're letting yourself in for?!

The answer may be 'yes', but if you're reading this book, we're presuming it's at least a partial 'no'! As the saying goes, 'you don't know what you don't know', and the only way you'll find out what you don't know is by immersing yourself in the subject. So read some more books, search the web for information and, importantly, speak to other investors about how they tackled the process. Ask what things took them by surprise when they carried out their first renovation and/or refurbishment work and what they've learned to do better. Question them about the pitfalls and ask for advice on how you can do the best job possible. You can do all the 'paper' research you like, but there's no substitute for real-life experiences, many of which we'll be sharing throughout this book.

One husband and wife team we're working with at the moment are absolutely bowled over by how fast we're working and the level of communication we have with them and with our team. Renovating and refurbishing a rental property is a major commercial project, run in an almost military style, and when most first-time investors have only ever carried out works on their own home, it's quite a shift in mindset.

Do you know why you're doing this?

That might sound like an odd question, but we're always amazed at how many investors don't have a clear plan for their projects. What's your end-game, both in the short and long term? By that we mean:

a)   what do you intend to do with the property once it's renovated and refurbished, and

b)   what's your exit strategy?

Property is just another money-making vehicle for us. What you ultimately want out of it (income or capital lump sum/s) and when (on completion of the project / on-going / in ten years / when you retire, etc.) will dictate what you buy and how you renovate and refurbish it, according to your target market, i.e. what kind of property, let in what kind of way will give you the return you're looking for?

So decide what your goals are and then spend some time carrying out specific local research. Use the internet to assess prices and demand (rightmove.co.uk and zoopla.co.uk have some great data you can access) and speak to local sales and letting agents to get their expert opinions on what people are looking for and how much they're willing to pay for it. Only then will you be able to decide what kind of end product you need to provide and what's going to stack up financially for you.

Are you prepared for the commitment you're taking on?

Anything that requires time, effort and money is a big commitment, personally, emotionally and financially. Investments always carry an element of risk and property is widely considered a 'medium' risk. If the amount of money you're putting in represents a large proportion of your overall capital savings, then the level of risk for you is probably higher than if you had a bigger 'cushion' behind you. And your attitude to this financial risk – potentially putting your own and your family's future security on the line - will affect you emotionally. We'll look at this in more detail in the next chapter.

If you're very hands-on with the project, it's going to take a lot of your time and you'll have to make sacrifices in your personal life. Hours that you might have spent watching your favourite shows, socialising and relaxing are highly likely to be given over to this project – are you prepared to knuckle down for as long as it takes? And, if there's a problem, are you in a position with what may be your other full-time job to be able to address urgent issues? If you have a salaried position with set working hours, you may find it hard to run a renovation and refurbishment project simultaneously, so think carefully about how much time you are, realistically, going to be able to dedicate to it.

Are you supported?

Following on from the previous point, make sure the people around you are also fully behind you. Your family and close friends are going to have to be supportive and understanding at various points and in equal measure, so talk to your nearest and dearest about what you're doing and be honest with them about how much time you're going to spending working and the extra pressure it might put on both you and them.

But it's not all misery! Share your enthusiasm, tell them when you've made good progress and then, when it's all over, you can celebrate with them properly and thank them for being there for you. Property investing can be a lonely and stressful business at times, so having the support of those closest to you will really make a difference.

Are you a decisive person?

Can you make a decision when you need to, or do you find yourself often thrown by having too many choices and tend to spend ages going back and forth? In this business there is a constant stream of options and decisions and you need to be able to, relatively quickly and painlessly, separate the wheat from the chaff, make a choice and move on. If you can't, you'll find your projects painful and stressful – and so will everyone around you!

We don't always make the very best decisions all of the time, but nobody's perfect. As long as you've carried out some good research and been diligent in checking out several available options, you can be pretty confident that it's at the very least a 'good' decision. Could you have made a better one? Perhaps – and you can improve on it when you carry out your next project.

How do you handle problems?

No matter how well you prepare and execute tasks and decisions, problems will arise. Property investment is a business littered with things beyond your control – tenant behaviour, forces of nature, market fluctuations – and the renovation and refurbishment process has its own share. Contractors will sometimes let you down; there may be an underlying problem within the structure of the property that didn't come up on your survey; supplies to the property may not be quite as sound as you thought; human error can occur; there may be an unavoidable delay with suppliers…and so it goes on. You need to accept that Sometimes Things Just Happen and, as with the previous point, you need to be able to assess what's happened, make a decision and move on.

So this is one of the key abilities you need to develop and a skill you need to hone if you're going to get involved in any project similar to this. It's the nature of the beast that hurdles will appear in your way and whether you succeed or not comes down to how you handle them. We've noticed that all successful investors have a common character trait where they almost relish issues and have creative responses ready to go. That's obviously something that comes with experience, but you need to try and fast-track yourself, mentally, and approach obstacles not just with a 'can-do' attitude, but also think ahead and anticipate those obstacles.

We were recently handling a project for a client where, once the sale had been agreed and we'd asked the council's HMO Officer to visit the property, she informed us that the kitchen was too small to comply with amenity standards. We knew immediately that we had two options: either take a wall down or to build on a conservatory.

The wall would have cost £5k; the conservatory £3k, in addition to which, we knew that if we laid the appropriate foundations underneath the conservatory, that would be the groundwork done for a possible double-storey extension in the future. We were solving a problem in a value-oriented way.

What we're saying is, if you're the kind of person who gets flustered when things don't go to plan, you may find hands-on property investing tricky. But learning how to deal with problems more effectively is not hard if you put your mind to it, so it's worth having a look at some of the materials and courses that are out there. The one we'd recommend is a basic project management course called Prince2 (their website is prince2.com), which teaches you about the various aspects of managing a project, assessing and managing risk, and it's a really useful tool that you can use in many other aspects of your life.

Project management is about time, quality & cost and ensuring that triangle of elements is balanced, co-ordinated and managed effectively.

How are your admin and computer skills?

'Success' in the renovation and refurbishment business is defined as bringing in the project on time, on budget and up to standard and you can't judge any of that without a meticulously prepared initial financial plan and schedule of works. You need to be really organised and make sure quotes, invoices and receipts – of which there are a huge number! – are all correctly logged and filed, and you must be on top of the bank accounts and credit cards in and out of which all the money is flowing.

We try to keep it as simple as possible, so we and our team mainly use Excel spreadsheets to track all the money, time, activity and people. The only whizzy thing we use in addition is an 'illustrator' package (ours is compatible with Macs), into which we input all the information we gather, including photographs, and that helps us create the final 'landscape' for the project. You should be able to pick up a package like that for around £40, so it may be worth the investment if you're planning on carrying out multiple projects or, if like us, you end up carrying out projects for clients and want to be able to drag together information very quickly for progress reports.

However you record and store the information on your project, the most important thing is that your system makes sense to you. Don't be tempted to invest in a package that's counter-intuitive to the way you work – and we've tried a few like that! Many investors we speak to manage perfectly well with spreadsheets - you don't have to over-complicate things. You'll often need to access details and figures quickly, so it's important you're on top of everything all of the time and know exactly where to find the information you need.

If that doesn't sound like something you're good at or something you would enjoy, you might want to consider having someone else manage the project for you. You could have a personal assistant handle all the administration, but you need to understand the figures, the process and why the schedule is as it is and that's hard to do when you haven't prepared it yourself.

Again, there are courses and books that can help you become adept at all of this, but this business will be far easier for you to get stuck into if you're already organised, computer-literate and figure-savvy.

Do you have good people-management skills?

You're going to be dealing with a lot of different people throughout your project and it's important that you can not only communicate well and get on with them, but that you can keep everyone motivated and working to schedule. Property is a people business and by far the best way of getting things done is by making people want to work with and for you.

You need to be a good negotiator and reasonable; firm but approachable; clear and appreciative. You also have to be able to be the 'bad guy' when necessary and not hold back from getting rid of bad tradesmen or unreliable suppliers, and that requires self-assuredness and diplomacy. If you think any of that might be a struggle, again, it may be better for you to employ a project manager.

Are you ready for the buck to stop with you?

Most importantly - and you may think we're stating the obvious here - you need to understand that this property investment project is your business. You may employ other people to carry out various jobs but the buck stops with you. You need to be in control of the project all the way through and skill yourself up to handle it.

Ultimately, it's on your shoulders whether it's a roaring success or fails to perform as it should, so you must carry out due diligence every step of the way. We meet investors all the time who blame tradesmen, tenants, the market, bad luck....when the simple truth is that their property investment didn't succeed because of something/s they did or didn't do.

So that's the big question: are you ready to be entirely responsible for your own success?

You might think we're trying to put you off here, but that's not true. Renovating and refurbishing property is an exciting, rewarding and highly addictive process. When you stand back from the dust, bricks and mortar and compare the building you bought to the finished product, there's an immense feeling of pride and satisfaction. And, trust us, you'll want to do it all again.

DO

- **Ask lots of questions.** Talk to people who have achieved what you want to achieve and pick their brains.
- **Get yourself organised.** Brush up on your Excel skills, re-acquaint yourself with files and filing, get out your calculator and clear some office space!
- **Think about how comfortable you are with risk.** You're investing a lot of time, money and effort and there is a (very slim) chance it might not go quite to plan. Are you okay with that?
- **Research the market.** Know exactly what demand you're supplying.
- **Share your ideas and plans with those around you.** It makes the tricky days much easier and the good times a lot more fun!

DON'T

- **Overstretch yourself.** Are you absolutely sure you have the time and money to do this project yourself, properly?
- **Simply have faith that 'it'll be fine.'** You need to prepare thoroughly and then follow a process. You can't wing it.
- **Try to follow a system that doesn't make sense to you.** Ask people how they record and track figures, check out software that might help you, but it's not a 'one-size-fits-all' thing, so do what works for you.

Keep your first deal simple and take your time.

Chapter 2

Preparing your finances

Hopefully, you've already got your finances straight and this chapter should just be a little refresher. If, however, you haven't spent a huge amount of time thinking about exactly what you have at the moment and how you'd like your financial future to look, it's well worth reading one of the other books in our 'success' series, 'PROPERTY INVESTMENT SUCCESS', which looks at property compared to other investment vehicles and goes through the different ways you can invest in property to get different returns.

And if you haven't spoken to a financial advisor yet, make that your next move; even better, speak to a Wealth Manager, who can look at all your financial affairs and make sure that your investments complement each other and everything is working towards your financial goals, in the most profitable and tax-efficient way. That's likely to cost you more but, in our opinion, Wealth Managers are worth their weight in gold. Even if you already have a trusted accountant and are certain you know what you're doing, it's never a bad idea to get a second opinion.

The other person you absolutely must speak to – if your Wealth Manager isn't able to fulfil the role – is a property tax specialist. Tax efficiency in property investment comes down, in a large part, to how you split what's considered a 'revenue' cost item and what's considered 'capital' – essentially, is it something that's being carried out purely for the business of letting the property, or is it something that's an improvement, intended to increase the value? Some things are clearly one or the other, but there are quite a lot of instances where taking the right advice on what you purchase and how you allocate your expenditure can greatly reduce your tax liability, In short, don't scrimp on getting the right advice.

In this chapter, we're looking at the key financial elements you need to tackle – and this should all be done before you make an offer on a property. Far too many people find what they think is a bargain, or a 'great deal', believing that they can't lose, without having run any real figures. This is purely and simply a financial move you're making, so the decision as to whether a property is worth buying relies on a huge number of factors, including:

- The purchase price versus its real market value
- The amount of capital investment required
- Price growth projections for the area
- Current rental values
- Detailed income and expenditure projections for your particular type of rental
- The mortgage rate you can secure

Gathering this information requires a good knowledge of the property investment business, a detailed level of research and some careful budgeting, with best and worst-case scenarios. You need to be as sure as you can that even if things don't go according to 'plan A', you won't be left out of pocket, having to subsidise your mortgage repayments yourself, or, in the worst case, end up in negative equity, potentially having the property repossessed and losing all your investment. If you prepare your finances correctly, none of that should happen!

Researching property values and rents

There's a lot of detail about researching areas, property capital values and rent rates in two of Nick's other books, 'HMO PROPERTY SUCCESS' and 'THE SECRETS OF BUY TO LET SUCCESS', both available via nickfox.co.uk and Amazon.co.uk; suffice to say here, you need to do a thorough job. If your budget is going to be useful to you, the figures you're putting down for rental income and projected value, both before and after the project, must be realistic. For everything you do in your budget, you should know best and worst-case values and prices, and therefore what a reliable 'middle ground' is.

Look online, speak to agents and get out there and have a look at some properties, so you get a real understanding of what something at X price looks and feels like. As we said in Chapter 1, if this project is to be successful and financially beneficial to you, you have to immerse yourself in your local property market, so make sure you become an expert on prices and values.

Buy To Let mortgages

The two most important things to say about buy to let mortgages are:

1. Consult an independent mortgage broker. You need to know that the person you're talking to can access every product available to you in the market and that they're not restricted or biased in any way.
2. When you meet with your broker, go armed with a thorough personal financial statement and clear investment plan. Only by knowing exactly how much capital you have access to and what you want out of your investment, can a financial professional help you secure the right product for you.

It's a huge marketplace and there are thousands of mortgage products, but you may be restricted by how you intend to let the property (mortgages for HMOs in particular have very specific criteria), the condition of the property you want to buy and the type of work you're planning to carry out. And the type of mortgage that's best for you, in terms of deal/rate tie-ins and whether you go for interest only or repayment, will depend on your own reasons for investing and financial plans. A great mortgage deal for one investor may not suit another, which is why you need to take advice that's tailored specifically to you and your situation.

At the time of writing, the market for financing HMOs is a very small one and product rates currently range from 3.17% to 6%. Although there aren't many lenders in this type of investment space, the ones that there are really understand what you're doing, so the actual application shouldn't be too painful for you!

We're often asked by clients whether there's any possibility of getting advance financing for building works, or whether they're likely to have retentions until any works are completed. The answer to both questions is 'no'. Most of the time when you're embarking on an HMO project, you're either buying an existing HMO to improve and upgrade, or you're converting a three-to-five bedroom family home. These tend to involve, at most, a few stud walls, perhaps the conversion of a garage or the addition of a conservatory or ground floor extension – things that aren't considered major building works by lenders.

We said it at the start of the chapter but, to reiterate: you must make sure you have funding in place before you start the project, so consult a broker at the earliest stage of your planning.

Investment Key Performance Indicators

Understanding the industry lingo and being able to analyse your figures accordingly will enable you to look at any potential investment and see not only whether it will give you the returns you want and need, but also to compare your proposed investment with others on a like-for-like basis. Once you know how to calculate Return on Investment (ROI), gross and net profit and gross and net yield, you'll be able to see whether you're keeping up with (and ideally exceeding) local market averages and how well your property/portfolio is performing against other types of investment. In short, you need to prove to yourself that a renovation and refurbishment project is the most appropriate place for you to put your capital. So here are those KPIs explained:

Return on Investment (ROI)

The ROI tells you what percentage of your invested capital is coming back to you each year in profit. The higher the ROI, the harder your money is working for you and the 'better' the investment. It's calculated by dividing your profit by your total capital investment (deposit, buying costs, refurbishment, furnishing, etc.). If you're intending to sell a property immediately after refurbishment, then it will be the profit you realise after selling and taking all the associated costs away. If you intend to keep the property and rent it out, you will calculate an annual ROI figure using the total annual rental profit. Clearly, in order to be able to do this, you need a clear and realistic projected income and expenditure budget.

For example:

Total capital investment	£75,000
Profit from sale (pre-tax)	£30,000 = 40% ROI
Annual rental profit from HMO	£12,000 = 16% ROI

And in case you're thinking that it looks far better to 'flip' the property in this situation, remember that you're getting this 16% every year from renting it out. In addition, because there has been capital growth, you may well be able to re-mortgage at some point and pull out some, if not all of your capital invested, which would increase the ROI accordingly.

This is the key figure that will allow you to compare your investment with others.

Gross and net profit
This is the annual rental profit figure mentioned above. Quite simply, your net profit is your rental income less your costs. You should also include an allowance for void periods (when the property/room is vacant) of around 5% and also for maintenance. We'll go into this in more detail in the next section, 'Putting together a budget'.

Your gross profit is simply your rental income, but this is not terribly useful, as costs are unavoidable but can vary significantly. This is one reason it's worth doing the best renovation and refurbishment job you can: so that you keep on-going maintenance costs as low as possible.

Gross and net yield

Yield is probably the figure you'll hear property investors talk about the most. It's also used by lots of companies selling investment deals, because they can make their headlines look good by mentioning fantastic yields, but keeping it very quiet that it's a gross figure, which is about as relevant as a gross profit figure. The only time gross yield is useful is in giving you a picture of which areas might have better returns, in terms of total annual rental income against the property value; otherwise it's fairly irrelevant, especially if you're trying to compare a property owned outright to one that is heavily mortgaged.

So, net yield is the annual net profit divided by the property's value, for example:

Property value	£200,000
Annual rental profit	£12,000
Net yield	6%
Annual rental income (before costs are deducted)	£26,000
Gross yield	13%

Once you've got all these KPI figures, you can then go out and make sure your investment in this project is a wise one, and you couldn't be making a better investment elsewhere. So, to make a start, you need a budget.

Putting together a budget, twice

This can't be stressed strongly enough: if you don't get this bit right, you could end up with, at best, a few unexpected costs and, at worst, a disaster of an investment. We're calling it a budget, but it's really more of an investment viability analysis, and we'd recommend doing it on an Excel spreadsheet.

It needs to show your income and expenditure, together with details of the property value, capital investment and mortgage repayment. You must also make sure you include allowances for voids and maintenance.

You're unlikely to find two investors who do their budgets and analysis in exactly the same way, but everyone will have more or less the same content. If you go to nickfox.co.uk and click on 'FREE STUFF', you can download a template; in the meantime, here are some of the key things you need to include:

Property details & initial capital input:
- The property's current value & a suggested purchase price

- Deposit required
- All buying costs
- Renovation & refurbishment costs (total from separate spreadsheet – see below)
- The cost of any mortgage repayments you'll need to make before the property can be tenanted

Projected monthly income:
- Your anticipated rental income
- Any other income (charges for washing machines or perhaps letting an outbuilding)

Projected monthly expenditure:
- Mortgage repayment amount
- Any utility or other property bills
- Maintenance costs
- Allowance for voids
- Management costs, if not doing it yourself

Renovation & refurbishment budget

This works here for your viability analysis and then together with your schedule of works (Chapter 5). On a separate spreadsheet, put together as detailed a list as you can of costs/expenditure required for the works and furnishing you'll be doing. The more detailed you make it, the more useful it will be to you, both on this project and in the future. Obviously, until you've actually secured a property, these figures will only be approximate, but research suppliers and talk to other local investors and get as accurate idea as you can of what are reasonable prices for labour and materials, etc. More detail about fixtures and fittings can be found in Chapter 8.

Very importantly, ALWAYS include a contingency. Things can change and problems can crop up and even the best-prepared budgets include a little wiggle room. We'd suggest allowing an additional 10% of the total cost you calculate for the renovation and refurbishment, so you don't hit a bump and find yourself short of funds. As standard, that's the amount we allow when we're putting together the first budget draft. Once the property has been properly inspected and the schedule of works drawn up, we pull the contingency down to 5% in the final budget. With every property, you tend to find issues that the survey didn't bring up - perhaps a flat roof is found to be leaking or there's some asbestos to dispose of – and it only takes a couple of things to eat into that contingency.

Only once you've been able to put all this information together in a budget will you be able to calculate your KPIs and see how well the investment project stacks up. Then you can start tinkering with the figures, seeing what changes or cutbacks you might need to make in order to get the returns you need and also how your proposed purchase would be performing compared to local averages. The more detailed your budget and analysis, the better you'll be able to see what you need to buy and how much it's worth spending on it in each case.

The first time you do the figures, you might feel like your head can't take it, but once you're clear on what you're doing and why, the next project will be far easier. As you go along, you'll tweak, refine and improve your analysis and, at the same time, you'll begin to recognise more quickly whether a property's worth taking on.

How we do it

We now have a pretty slick system for sourcing viable properties. Every week, two of us go out and view around ten properties that we've picked from an online assessment of 30-35 possibilities, where we've ruled out ones that don't meet basic criteria. For example, if any bedroom has a dimension of under seven feet it won't work; if any room doesn't have natural light, it's out. If we like one, we'll have a quick walk around to get a feel for the spec and an idea of how we could divide the space; things such as where we're going to put en-suites, where the soil stack is so that we don't have to use macerators and pumps, etc.

We then have a good chat with the vendor, go through our checklist and start to put together our statement of works: do we need a boiler and/or megaflow hot water cylinder, do we need stud walls, en-suites, and so on? Back at the office, we input everything into our software illustrator package, including all the photographs we've taken, to create a real landscape of the project scheme. It quickly generates the information we need to know about the extent and cost of works, the rents we'll be able to charge and gives us the bottom line figures: the monthly profit and the ROI. (See Chapter 5 for more information on compiling all your property information.)

And we're quite regimented in our decision on whether to make an offer. We look for at least £1,000 pre-tax profit per month and a minimum 12% ROI. If the schedule of works and income/ expenditure projections stack up to satisfy those two bottom lines, our project is a go-er.

DO

- Have a clear financial statement, showing all your assets, liabilities, income and expenditure.
- Speak to an Independent Financial Advisor or Wealth Manager.
- Take specialist tax advice from someone who understands property investment and buy to let.
- Make sure you understand your KPIs and budget correctly. None of this is worthwhile doing if you can't assess how well your property project stacks up against other investment options.
- Include a 10% contingency in your initial budget.

DON'T

- Forget to make sure your capital is accessible. A project can be lost through capital not being available in time.

And, very importantly...

DON'T forget to put a value on your own time. We say it over and over: there are too many investors who think they're saving money by doing things themselves that actually turn out to be false economy. Every hour that you're working on this project is an hour you could be doing something else and you need to look at the cost of getting someone else to carry out the work versus the value to you of having that time to yourself – whether you used to earn more in your 'day job' or simply think it's more valuable to you to be able to spend more time with your partner. Keep track of how long you spend on the project so that when it's over, you can look at your returns and profit and decide how worthwhile all the investment of your time has been. Your time is a KPI too.

If you have any queries about how to find good advisors for your property investment business, just email hello@nickfox.co.uk and we'll be happy to point you in the right direction.

Chapter 3

Preparing for the legal bits

Buy to let is full of legal requirements and regulations, some of which can feel as though they're getting in the way of your project, but it really is important you adhere to all of them. And you can't adhere to something you don't know about, so this is where you really need to make sure you dot the 'i's and cross the 't's, as the legal pitfalls of renovation and refurbishment can be deep - expensive and with serious repercussions. Most relate to planning, building standards and health and safety and, while some are national regulations, many can vary from area to area, so the first place you need to acquaint yourself with is your local council office.

And that's a little more time-consuming than you might have hoped, because departments rarely share information, meaning you have to liaise and build separate relationships with each one. There's really no way around this, but if you make a good job of it with your first project, your second should be a whole lot more straightforward.

If you're not used to dealing with these kinds of legalities and processes – and particularly if you've never had to work with your local council - many of the conversations you have with council representatives and planning professionals will feel frustrating, because it's very tricky to get anything in writing. Of course, all your formal applications will be acknowledged in black and white, but final decisions will take time to come through and, nine times out of ten, what you're looking for is an immediate yes or no! So, successfully navigating your way through the early stages, where nothing can actually be put in writing because you may not have a property yet, becomes heavily reliant on you laying the groundwork and building good relationships with the people who have the answers – or at the very least an informed, 'inside' opinion. You need to get yourself to the point where they understand what you want to do, you understand what you need to do for them and you know that they'll give you as reliable an indication as possible as to whether you're likely to get a yes or a no in a particular situation.

If we're making it all sound a bit 'grey', that's because it is. Of course, there are certain things you have to do and certain things you can't do, but much depends on how well you explain and provide supporting materials for your plans; much is dependent on the market conditions at the time you submit your paperwork and much is dependent on how the person making the decision feels on the day. It's a bit like taking an exam: if you've done your homework properly, there shouldn't be any surprises, but nothing is guaranteed.

The good news is that you're one step ahead of the game reading this! Here are the key legal pools you're going to be wading through during the successful execution of your project, together with the main points you need to consider and how best to address them.

Planning permission

Planning doesn't only relate to new buildings, conversions and extensions; it also covers change of use. This is of particular relevance if your project is the conversion of a single-household home or block of units into an HMO, as the rules governing change of use from one 'class' of housing to another (primarily C3 to C4) changed in 2010.

The national law states that a property will simply automatically change class as it changes use but, in practice, that's rarely the case. And that's because each local Planning Authority has the right to make an Article 4 Direction, which requires anyone wishing to let a property as an HMO to apply for planning permission. Many council areas have chosen to go down this route, as it enables them to ensure no one area becomes saturated with this particular type of accommodation. While that broadly makes sense, it does make things more difficult than they used to be for you, as an investor:

a) Before you commit to investing in an area, you need to check whether the local planning authority has an Article 4 Direction in place and find out, by speaking to them directly and talking to other local landlords, how they tend to rule.

b) If there is an Article 4 Direction in place, you could find yourself having to complete on a property before you've had planning approval for its use as an HMO signed off!

c) Because regulations are constantly shifting within the sector, you need to make sure you have the right contacts to keep up to date with any changes that might affect you.

So, if you're looking to let property as an HMO, make an appointment to see your local HMO Officer / Amenity Standards Officer (the title may differ between local authorities) to find out exactly what their HMO policy is and which areas it could prove tricky for you to invest into. These people are there to help you, so use them! Be up front about your intentions and ask for their advice, making it very clear that you're a professional investor, looking to provide high-quality accommodation that helps fulfil the local housing needs in the best way.

If, in doing that, you're going to be extending or converting part of a property – which is highly likely – you also need to speak to the local Planning Officer to find out what kind of projects tend to be approved and which are usually turned down. The more specific you can be, the more seriously they'll take you, so make sure you've carried out proper research into the rental demands of the area and can demonstrate that your plans are intended to satisfy those demands.

Most of the work we do in our renovation projects falls under 'permitted development', which mean you don't need to make a planning application. Loft conversions or changing a garage into a room, for example, are usually permitted development but, as with so much of the legislation around property, it does vary between councils.

We always get in touch with the local council planning office prior to purchase, to discuss our plans and check what's within permitted development. For any proposed works that fall outside that, we find out about the likelihood of planning being granted, so we know at the earliest stage what changes we may need to make to our schedule of works.

For example, last year, we had agreed the purchase of a fairly modern property that we wanted to convert into an HMO, but the local planner wouldn't allow a carport to be built up and converted into a room. The reasoning was that it would remove a parking space for the property, something that's often an issue with newer properties, particularly if they're within an estate. Not being able to convert the carport took our plan down from a six to a five-bedroom HMO. Fortunately, we were able to add a single-storey extension to the rear so that the figures still stacked up, however, that could easily not have been the case.

In addition to the council planners, you should also be able to find freelance planners to advise and act for you. They tend to be people who used to work for the local council and who therefore know how the system works and who to go to within the council to get the answers you need. You will need to pay for their services, but it may be worth the investment for peace of mind and to have someone who can expedite any planning applications for you.

Building Regulations

Hand in hand with Planning Permission comes Building Regulations. Most aspects of your refurbishment project will require the approval of a Building Control Officer / Building Inspector, who will work with you and your contractors to make sure all the work is up to standard. As with HMO Officers, these people have an advisory role and are there to help you, although you will have to pay for their services – usually somewhere between £400 and £800, depending on the extent of the works and number of inspections required.

We sit down with the Building Control Officer as soon as we start the project and show them what we're planning to do. We agree a fee for a series of inspections that will take place at various stages of the project, creating a Building Notice, which includes a final inspection for sign-off. At the end of the project, you'll be given a certificate to say everything's been done correctly, giving you peace of mind that there won't be any come-back at a later date.

Soundproofing within HMOs is not something that's required as standard, but it has come up a few times as an issue for Building Control in certain local council areas. This is something that can cost tens of thousands to rectify if you have to install it retrospectively, so make it very clear how you intend to let the property and ask the officer the question about soundproofing, even if they don't bring it up.

Health & Safety

Much of this concerns fire safety, so, if your HMO / Amenity Standards Officer can't advise you, have a conversation with your local Fire Safety Officer. Every fire department should have someone who will happily advise you, completely free of charge, as to what you need to do to be compliant. Explain to them how you intend to let the property out and they'll be able to give you guidance about what you should install in the way of:

- Fire alarms
- Smoke detectors & heat sensors
- Fire doors
- Fire extinguishers & blankets
- Exit signs and other signage
- Windows at the correct level to provide escape routes
- Emergency lighting.

How much of the above you're legally required to do will depend on whether your property falls under HMO licensing legislation.

But, regardless of what the law dictates, it's always best to err on the side of caution. Lettings legislation is constantly being amended and updated, so try to stay one step ahead by going the extra mile right from the start. Installing these safety measures is much easier to do at the renovation and refurbishment stage than at a later date.

You will also need to carry out a fire safety risk assessment, analysing the potential hazards in the property and declaring that every reasonable step has been taken to avoid them. There's nothing to say you couldn't do this yourself, but we wouldn't advise it, unless you can prove you've been properly trained in fire safety. This is a document that you might need to rely on, should anything happen to one of your tenants in the future and they accuse you of negligence. Paying a couple of hundred pounds to have a professional complete the assessment for you is money well spent, in our opinion.

The other thing you need to look into, particularly if you're going to be splitting rooms and putting up stud walls or converting spaces into bedrooms, is the minimum room size requirement. Your HMO Officer or someone from the Housing Standards department will be able to advise you on how many square meters you need to provide as a minimum in order for a room to qualify as single or double, and they'll also give you guidance on the amount of cooking, refrigeration and washing facilities you should be providing, according to the number of tenants you intend to house.

Again – and we're going to keep saying this! – standards will vary between councils. The information will be available on their website, so start off by looking there, so that when you do speak to someone in the department, you're already armed with some knowledge and can demonstrate that you're keen to make sure you're compliant.

We've heard lot of horror stories about people who'd mistakenly thought they could save themselves a lot of aggravation by 'flying under the radar' with the local council but, in almost every case, they ended up losing time and money through having to retrospectively comply with planning, building or health and safety regulations. It's really not worth the risk and, with the private rental sector continuing to grow, you really need to make sure you're above board with everything you do, so that you can confidently charge a good level of rent.

Landlord accreditation

Currently, there is no legal requirement for landlords in England to be either registered or accredited/qualified in any way. However, given that landlords in Scotland and Wales do now need to register themselves and/or their properties in order to let legally, we're of the opinion that similar legislation is likely to hit England in some form in the next few years. So we'd recommend you check with your local landlord's association whether they offer any kind of accreditation. Sometimes the checks made on you for accreditation are not particularly thorough, but we'd always suggest you show willing.

Also, check with your HMO Officer or Amenity Standards that you're on any register they might have for HMOs. This is something quite separate from licensing and most councils will make a note to carry out inspections every few years, just to check that your fire safety standards and amenities continue to meet the minimum requirements.

Insurance

At the point at which you exchange contracts, you will need to have buildings insurance in place, and that's the case regardless of whether it's residential or buy to let. However, as a landlord you will need specialist landlord insurance and, if you're letting an HMO, you're likely to be very limited in your choice of providers. We use 'block insurance', where we have one policy that covers our entire portfolio of properties and every time we buy a new one, we just add it in. It's cost-effective and cuts down on the admin, which, in itself, saves money.

The important thing with insurance is to communicate exactly how you'll be renting the property out and make sure that you're covered for absolutely everything you might need. As a landlord, in addition to standard property concerns such as fire, flooding, theft and accidental damage, you should certainly be asking about cover for:

- Professional indemnity (protecting you against any claims that might be made by tenants, visitors or contractors for personal injuries sustained in the property)
- Malicious damage by tenants
- Re-housing costs (giving tenants somewhere else to live while any repairs are taking place)
- Rent guarantee insurance.

And speak to your insurer about the planned works and how long they'll take to complete, because they will want to note when various stages are taking place, when the property is occupied, how it's secured during works, etc., and they might want to come out and inspect the property. They may even ask to see your schedule of works. In short, be very open about what you're doing and volunteer as much information as you can, because the last thing you want is for something to go wrong during your project and to find out you're not covered because of something you failed to declare to your insurer.

In addition, you MUST make sure that your contractors have their own appropriate public liability insurance. Some will also hold professional indemnity insurance that covers their work, and you need to check their health & safety process – how do they ensure the site is safe and can they demonstrate that they're working in a safe way? We'll come on to checking credentials and go into more detail in the next chapter...

DO

- Present yourself as a professional 'career' investor. Show you understand the local market and intend to provide high-quality accommodation that complies absolutely with letting regulations and exceeds expectations.
- Make sure you can demonstrate that your project will satisfy local demand. When speaking to the local council, show that your project has a clear purpose and will be beneficial to the area.
- Speak to local Amenity Standards / HMO, Planning and Building Control Officers at the earliest opportunity.
- Be very clear with your insurer about what you're doing and when.

DON'T

- Put any offers in until you've spoken to the council to find out what you can and can't do. The last thing you want to do is end up with a property you can't transform into the money-making vehicle you'd planned on having.
- Scrimp on paying for planning and building control advice. Doing a good job of building relationships with these professionals from day one will pay dividends in the future.

Tip…

You will be able to view and/or download both the minimum amenity standards and fire safety standards from your local council website, under the section on Private Sector Housing / HMOs.

Chapter 4

Preparing your team

Having a good, reliable team to carry out the work for you is probably the most important factor in the success of the project, after your financial budgeting. Remember the 'triangle' of time, quality and cost that we mentioned in Chapter 1? If any of your team of contractors, suppliers and professional advisors doesn't do their job properly, all three of those things are affected. In this business, you're relying a great deal on other people doing what they say they can do, when they've said they'll do it, to the standard you require and at the price they've quoted. When you take those four requirements and multiply them by the number of people on your team, that's a lot of risk.

So preparing your team is about two key things: finding the right people to work with and establishing a great line of communication with those people. It's about researching their credentials, making it very clear what you expect from them, right from the start, and then managing them in such a way that you get the best out of them. You might not get it right the first time and you will almost certainly have to let people go and find better replacements every now and then, but that's just another one of the hurdles this business throws at you. The key is being able to deal with it and move on.

Good property tax advisor

Everyone on your team is important, but a good property tax advisor is the person who can ultimately make a very big difference to the profitability of your investment, year after year. The renovation and refurbishment stage, which involves probably the greatest capital outlay you'll make on the property, is where your expenditure really needs to be allocated in the right way. We'd suggest that only someone who is both highly qualified AND has years of experience of handling the tax affairs of buy to let investors can advise you properly.

And this is someone you ideally want to engage before you buy any properties, because they'll also be able to advise you on the best way to own your investment/s, depending on what returns you want from them and when, to suit your income, capital, inheritance and retirement planning.

Where do I find this person?

Take recommendations from other investors, ask around at your local landlords association....your independent financial advisor should also be able to give you some recommendations. Ideally, choose someone who's an investor themselves – preferably with HMOs or, at the very least, with clients who have HMOs. You want to engage someone who knows exactly what they're doing and if it costs you a little more than you'd hoped, we'd suggest that paying extra for the additional expertise is probably worth it.

Pro-active mortgage broker

This may be a mortgage broker, it may be an independent financial advisor, but whoever is arranging your mortgage for you, make sure that they're completely independent and can access every product available. It's also hugely important that they're pro-active and will keep you informed about any upcoming changes to your product, anticipate when fixed rate or discounted periods are coming to an end, and always be on the lookout for a better product. You should be speaking to your broker around once every six months, just to make sure everything's in order and to get their thoughts on how the market might shift in the next 6-12 months. Your mortgage repayment is your biggest monthly cost, so making sure you're always on the best available rate can really make a difference to your on-going profits.

Local authority officers

As we said in the previous chapter, you should build good relationships within the relevant departments at your local council and consider them part of your wider team. The three key people you need to have on your side are:

- Planning Officer
- HMO / Amenity Standards Officer
- Building Control Officer / Building Inspector

With each of them, it's important that you present yourself as professional and informed – the easier you can make it for them to deal with you, the more willing they'll be to help you out when you need it. So have to hand simple copies of your schedule of works, together with sketches and any other pertinent details of the property. Make sure you've looked at the local council website and spoken to other local landlords before you meet with these council officers, so that you have a fairly good idea of what they're going to say and can prepare specific questions.

These people are there to help you achieve a good standard of work and provide high-quality rental accommodation. They're not trying to be deliberately awkward – remember, there is still a huge undersupply of private rental sector properties, so they want you to invest in the area – so if they're asking for certain things to be done a certain way, it's because they're looking to maintain standards. And be pro-active when you speak to them. Don't just find out what you're obliged to do and what the minimum standards are, ask them their opinion on what they think would be ideal. Show them you're keen to exceed expectations for quality and safety and they'll be keen to encourage you in return.

The caveat to the above is that sometimes you need to stand your ground. For example, you might be told that you need to put a washbasin in each room, or that a second cooker is required when, really, common sense tells you that it's just not necessary. As much of the amenities advice is guidelines, rather than law, you can often argue your case successfully – provided that you have a good relationship with the officer and can show that you've taken every step to comply with all the legal requirements, going over and above in some cases.

Essentially, you need to demonstrate that you understand the local authority regulations and guidelines and make them see that you want to work with the various council departments to help raise the standard of accommodation in the private rented sector. Some of that is down to research and preparation; some is down to your interpersonal skills, so make sure you've done all you can to hone both.

Contractors

It's really important you get your team of contractors right, because they have to work together. Over the course of the renovation and refurbishment project, things have to be done in a certain order and if one of the tradespeople is running behind, it can throw out your schedule of works (see the next chapter), plus, if the team don't get on with each other, it makes for a bad atmosphere and negative behaviours. We'll come on to talking about managing the team shortly, but, when you're selecting your contractors, bear in mind that it's not just the quality of their work and price you're looking at, but their overall reputation for having a good attitude on site.

These are the key players you'll need on the team, together with the associations and/or trade bodies they should belong to:

- Builder / Lead contractor (ideally, someone who can also project manage), preferably a member of the Federation of Master Builders (FMB)
- Plumber, Gas Safe registered
- Electrician, 'Part P' registered
- Plasterer, preferably a member of the Federation of Plastering and Drywall Contractors (FPDC)
- Painter/decorator, preferably a member of the Painting and Decorating Association (PDA)
- Glazer, FENSA member
- Locksmith, ideally from the Master Locksmiths Association
- Carpet fitter
- Cleaner.

Where do I find these people?
Checkatrade.com is a great source and take recommendations from other local property professionals. Your suppliers will also be able to give you leads, so keep asking around and you'll find the same names will come up. Then it's a case of meeting face to

face to talk through what you'll need and ask to see examples of their work. And if someone's busy, that's good – always be wary of a contractor who doesn't yet know you but seems to be able to do anything you want as soon as you want it!

Although we've already mentioned it above, we just want to stress how important it is that before you engage any contractor, you check their registration with a relevant organisation / trade body and that they have the appropriate insurance. You must be sure that if anything goes wrong or you're not happy with their work, you have some kind of recourse. If you've taken recommendations and testimonials, you shouldn't find yourself with any cowboys, but do double-check online that they really are paid-up members of the bodies they say they are.

Managing the team

You may be tempted to project manage the refurbishment yourself, but I'd highly recommend you employ someone else to do it. The refurb contractors need to be able to work together – if they all have their own agendas, you can find projects stall or take longer than necessary because they're all blaming each other for not being able to get on to the next stage. A project manager (often a general builder) will usually have a regular team that he knows will work efficiently together and you pay him extra to make sure everything stays on track. It also means you only have one person to liaise with.

Right at the start of the project, we get all the trades together for a meeting on site and go through everything on the schedule of works to make sure the whole team's clear on what they're doing and the fact that the lead builder is responsible for the day-to-day management of the process. You'll still need to be on site regularly yourself to check everything's going as it should; this is your project and it's ultimately your responsibility to make sure the team is happy, working to standard and there aren't any problems, so don't think you can put your feet up until the project manager says it's all done!

In terms of getting the team to work well for you, it's quite simple: pay them on time and be considerate, be human. Our team get regular work, we give them 40% up front and pay stage payments when they're due. We don't mess them around and usually arrive on site with sandwiches, biscuits and a good sense of humour. Yes, you need to keep things moving along and address problems, but remember these are just people earning a living, like you, so treat them well.

Suppliers

In the main, your contractors will provide their own materials and will certainly be able to recommend suppliers that they're familiar with for the fixtures and fittings you'll need to choose. However, it's always worth getting further quotes and looking at other suppliers. As with much of this business, there will be certain places that are used to supplying buy to let properties, so you'll probably get the most appropriate recommendations from other local landlords and the contractors who are used to working with them.

We let all our tradesmen get their own materials – it's much easier that way. However, you do need to make sure that they know to break down all the materials and labour and list them separately on their invoices. Your tax advisor can't do their job properly if the figures aren't where they should be.

Remember also that if you're going to be furnishing a property, some items may need to be ordered and could have a long lead time, so make sure you find out how long things like bathroom suites, beds and sofas might take to arrive. The last thing you want is to have the fabric of your property all ready to go and beautifully decorated, then end up paying the mortgage for another month because you can't tenant your HMO unfurnished!

Utility providers

They're not, strictly speaking, part of your team, but they are important suppliers and choosing the right provider/s can really make your life – and your tenants' lives – a lot easier. We use a company that specialises in shared housing and supplies all our utilities (energy, water, phone/broadband & TV licence) under one umbrella. The huge benefit is that there's a single bill per month, per property, which cuts down massively on admin, leaving only the council tax on top to worry about. You don't want multiple bills on same property - that's just an unnecessary time and money overhead - so we'd strongly recommend going with a specialist provider like this.

Letting agent

If you're intending to use a letting agent, you must include them in your project and ask for their advice. In carrying out your initial research into local demand, you'll probably find you click with one agent more than others; not every agent really understands buy to let and property as an investment, so you might need to speak to more than one person in a branch to get the information you need about yields and returns. Even if you're not planning to use a high street agent to let the property, or engaging a freelance property manager, it's still an idea to build a good relationship with someone local, who can help you stay on top of tenant demand, wants and needs.

When you do find someone who 'gets' what you're doing, be proactive in your communications with them. Letting agents often get a heads-up when landlords are selling, before properties go on the market, so let them know you'll view on a phone call, without necessarily having seen details, always turn up and always call them soon afterwards to give them your feedback.

Most good agents will be happy to help out local landlords, so tell them you'd really appreciate their advice. Show them the property at an early stage, check that your original research is still correct and find out exactly what tenants are currently looking for, in terms of décor, furnishings, etc. This doesn't change very much over time, but there may be something that the agent finds tenants are suddenly asking for, such as satellite television or more washing machines, and they'll be able to advise you as to what extra things you might be able to include that will make the rooms let more quickly and/or enable you to charge more rent. You can then go back to your budget and financial viability spreadsheet and see if it's worth doing.

In short…

…preparing your team is about research and communication. Be very clear on your goals and plans, take the time to find the right people for you and then communicate with them exactly what you need and expect. If you've prepared yourself properly, you shouldn't find this too difficult.

DO

- Check the credentials of your team. Sometimes people have let their certification or trade body membership lapse; sometimes they lie – you should be able to check them all out online.
- Be clear on what your project entails and what you need/expect from each person. Communication is key throughout your project.
- Be professional. Show the local authority you're a professional investor, have done your research and are properly prepared.
- Use an 'umbrella' utility provider. It'll make your life so much easier.

DON'T

- Try to manage the whole project yourself. Instructing a lead contractor, who's on site every day and probably has his own team he's used to working with, is by far the most sensible option.
- Be afraid to ask for help and advice. Most local property professionals are happy to share their expertise.

Chapter 5

Preparing your schedule of works

This is your framework for the project. It's where the budget, jobs and materials are broken down and a timescale is applied. It's your roadmap, your bible, your blueprint for the work, so it needs to be accurate.

Because we've been in the business for many years, our schedule of works is a slick beast! We have a standard template that can very quickly be tweaked and tailored to each project, but the timeframe rarely changes and our contractors know they will usually need to work to a 4 to 7-week plan. Everything is standardised – our suppliers, our materials, fixtures, fittings, furnishings and décor – so we can budget and plan the work very quickly, as soon as we know what renovation and refurbishment the property requires.

But that's us and where we are now. How should you start?

Your initial scheme and scope of work

The first thing you need to do is have a template – we just use a Word document – that you can complete as you walk around the property, noting all the work that's going to need doing. Below is a same scheme for 'Property A', showing the categories we use, together with example notes, so you can get an idea of how the schedule starts:

Property A

Scheme outline

Currently:

- 3 bedroom terrace, 1960s
- Small front and back gardens
- Large living room and dining room connected
- Not in good decorative order

Convert to 5-bed HMO with 2 en-suites, 1 exclusive use of upstairs bathroom and 2 sharing downstairs bathroom (extended from current WC into utility room):

- Ground floor: Stud walls to separate living room and dining area. New bathroom for downstairs rooms to share.
- 1st Floor: 2 doubles to include new en-suites and smaller room given exclusive use of 1st floor bathroom.

Plan of work

Fire systems

- Full system – smoke detectors in all common parts and heat sensor in kitchen
- Emergency lighting above and below staircase
- Fire doors (7) closers and smoke baffle / intumescent strips

Internal walls

- Stud walls to separate existing living room and dining room

Kitchen

- Full refurbishment required

Plumbing

- En-suites created in two 1st floor bedrooms
- New bathroom downstairs into utility room
- Some work in existing bathroom (new shower, etc.)

Wiring

- Full rewiring required

TV distribution and digital aerial supply

- To all rooms

Re-keying

- Locks and keys to all doors to be refitted using master keying system.

Internal Decoration

- Full refurbishment of internal decoration required
- Furnishing and curtains for all bedrooms, as required

External

- No external issues
- Gardens easy care
- Parking locally is reasonable

Furnishings, curtains and lampshades

- Standard pack

Certification

- Gas safety certificate
- Electrical certificate
- HMO certificate not required in this case
- Fire alarm commissioning certificate

Once this information has been gathered, you can cost up the works to get an overall refurbishment budget.

Works budget

The first time you do this, it'll take some time to get quotes and estimates, but if you do a good job on that first project, you'll have all the figures to hand for the future. Here's an example of costs we allocated to the fairly comprehensive refurbishment of Property A:

Itemised Improvement Costs

Kitchen	£3,500
En-suites	£7,000
2 bathrooms (existing plus new)	£6,000
Boiler & megaflow hot water cylinder	£4,200
Fire safety works	£3,990
Rewiring	£3,500
Stud walls	£1,500
Mortgage payments during refurb	£2,500
Redecoration	£2,000
Recarpet	£2,500
Furnishing & curtains	£5,200
Rekeying	£950
Misc. labour	£1,200
Project management	£5,000
Contingency 5%	£2,500
Total	**£51,540**

Obviously, the costs above are a total relating to each job, which are broken down into much more detail elsewhere. As we said before, you can go into as much or as little detail as you like in your price research – you could itemise it down to each screw, but that might be taking it a bit far! However, as an example, 'Fire safety works' above would be made up of costs for:

- fire doors
- intumescent strips
- fire door closers
- smoke alarms
- heat sensors
- fire blanket (kitchen)
- extinguisher (kitchen)

As mentioned earlier, we let our contractors source their own materials, so the costs shown also include labour. When you first start out, you should certainly separate the two very clearly, so that you can see exactly how the costs are divided, but as you go on, you'll get to the point where you just know, for example, that an en-suite costs £3,500 (to include stud walls, tiling, all fixtures & fittings, plumbing material costs and labour). Just don't forget that, for tax purposes, the two need to be clearly separated.

Once you have your works budget and know the exact capital input required, you can go back to your viability analysis and check that the investment still stacks up and your ROI figure means it makes financial sense to proceed.

The final schedule of works

So you have a complete list of jobs and works, along with a budget for the project; now you need to look at the timescale. We've said that our team work to a 4 to 7-week timeframe as standard and that's a pretty good guide for you. If you don't have much work to do, you may be able to do everything in a month; in terms of it taking longer than 7 weeks, that shouldn't really happen. Two months plus is becoming a pretty serious renovation, probably involving structural work, and that's simply not the kind of property we'd recommend for a buy to let investment where you want to keep the timescale between completion and ready to rent as tight as you can.

While you don't need to know every last detail, you do need to make sure you get a full picture of what work is involved, the jobs that need to be carried out and the order in which everything needs to be done. So ask your project manager / lead builder to sit down with you and go through a typical HMO refurbishment. Make it clear you're not going to be hanging over his shoulder the whole way through, but it is important for you to know that by the end of week two, for example, X should be completed and work on X should be beginning.

It's also helpful – to you and your contractors – to have a rough floor plan, showing the existing layout and the changes you're planning to make. Virtually every property for sale these days has a floor plan, so you can simply copy that, and mark on it things like stud walls, new en-suites and bathrooms and other reconfigured rooms. For your first project, you will probably find a sketch of each room useful as well, where you can mark on where radiators and sockets will be and perhaps where the furniture will be situated. It's entirely up to you – do what makes you feel comfortable and able to best communicate exactly what you want and need from your team.

Here are some sample floor plans that we put together on PowerPoint:

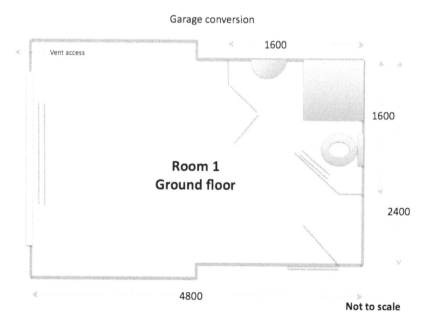

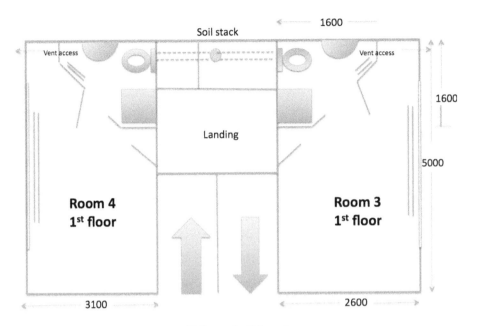

1st Floor refurbishment

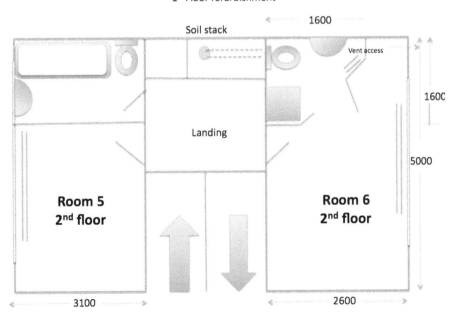

2nd Floor refurbishment

We said in the last chapter that problems can arise if one contractor starts blaming another's slow progress for not being able to get on with their next job and that's one of your project manager's main responsibilities: keeping everyone on schedule. And you can't assess whether he's doing his job properly if you don't know yourself what should be happening, so take some time to get it straight in your head and do a simple spreadsheet, broken down by days/weeks and jobs. If your tradespeople are very used to this kind of project, they should be pretty much bang on, but making it clear that you know more or less what they should be doing and when, means there's less chance of things slipping. Share this schedule with your team, get their feedback and make any tweaks, so you can be sure everyone's clear and on the same page right from the start.

We recently spoke to someone who'd had an absolute nightmare with her renovation project because she'd tried to manage everything herself, source all her own materials and had broken down every last cost. She'd spoken to her tradesmen in a huge amount of detail about the order in which they needed to do things and how long each task would take, and they really didn't understand why she needed to know. Her final spreadsheet of timescale and costs was so detailed it was virtually useless as a tool for effective management of the project, as none of the tradespeople could understand it! The project ended up overrunning because she managed to confuse her entire team, including herself; the materials she'd ordered never seemed to arrive at the right time and many of them were wrong; the team almost walked off the job because she was micro-managing to such an extent that it appeared she didn't trust them… it was probably the best example of why new investors shouldn't try to manage a whole project themselves!

Assuming you've chosen your contractors and tradespeople well, trust that they know what they're doing. Each of them has worked with other trades on projects numerous times and is used to communicating – plus, you have a lead contractor to project manage them for you - so don't bog yourself down with unnecessary detail.

We're all different in terms of the level of detail we're comfortable with, but you can waste a lot of time – as the lady in the example above did – concerning yourself with timescales and costs that really don't need to be broken down. On your first project, you'll undoubtedly find yourself wanting to do just that, because you want to know absolutely everything, but try to fight the urge!

Compile your information

You should now have everything you need to get started on your project. The software package we use condenses all the costs, budgets and analysis on the property and project into a PDF report that we send to our clients. That's obviously not something you necessarily need to do when it's your own project, but we'd advise you do something similar. That way, you have all your figures in one place for easy reference. You can download a FREE sample property report from nickfox.co.uk - here's a summary of what it contains:

- **Overview,** with purchase and mortgage figures, income and cash flow, plus KPIs
- **Full purchase analysis**, from which the Overview figures are taken, with capital input broken down, financial metrics, income and expenditure breakdown and various rate assumptions
- **Forward projections,** predicting income and expenditure for years 1-5, 10 and 25, plus scenarios for if you wanted to sell the property at various stages
- **Rent rates**
- **Itemised improvement costs** (as shown earlier in chapter)
- **Photographs of current condition.**

In terms of future projections, the report goes into quite some detail about loan rates, potential sale costs and values, and also includes graphs showing cash flow, anticipated market value and ROI. While you can use software packages to generate these figures, we'd recommend spending some time doing it yourself via spreadsheets, so that you really gain an understanding of how to calculate the way your project stacks up, both today and into the future. Once you understand that, you can move on to the short-cuts, if you wish – they certainly save time!

As far as all the background work for your analysis goes, Nick's first book, 'HMO PROPERTY SUCCESS', has lots of information on how to research rent rates, capital values, redecorating and furnishing costs, etc., so if you haven't already read it, you can buy a copy from nickfox.co.uk - and Nick will even sign it for you!

Finally, get yourself some storage

It's not quite 'works' but one thing it's a very good idea to do, particularly if you're intending to build a portfolio of several properties, is to organise some storage space. During works, things may be delivered before the property is actually ready to accommodate them, such as bathroom suites, kitchens or furniture, and you're going to have to house them somewhere.

So look into renting a garage or other similar unit (which is usually cheaper than a storage unit with Safestore, Big Yellow, etc.) and build that into your budget. It'll be really useful, not only during renovation and refurbishment, but also as your tenants change. Some people want to bring their own bed and some have property they'd like to store safely while they're with you – there are lots of situations where, as a landlord, having a decent storage space makes your life a lot easier – and you may be able to charge tenants a little extra as well.

DO

- Take lots of photographs. Check with the vendor/agent that it's okay, but there shouldn't be any problem. It's amazing what you forget once you leave a property.
- Get hold of a floorplan. It doesn't have to be to scale, but you need to be clear on what's where and on the way you're planning to divide the space.
- Check and double-check your figures. Do your research well and keep an eye on your KPIs.
- Take advice from your contractors. They'll have some reliable, cost-effective recommendations for you.
- Secure some storage space. Garages are ideal, but make sure they're watertight.

DON'T

- Bog yourself down with too many details. You need to know how much the project's going to cost, but you don't need to know the price of every pot of paint and exactly how long it'll take the plumber to fit the WC!
- Try to source all the materials yourself. Let your contractors get their own supplies and fittings where you can.
- Rush. Take time to put together your schedules and budgets – the success of the project relies heavily on the planning.

PART TWO:
THE PROJECT

Chapter 6

So you've found a property...

...let's have a re-cap. By the time you've found what you think could be a great investment, you should:

Know:
- you can do this!
- all your project costs
- that your investment stacks up
- your KPIs: profit, ROI, yield
- how long the project's going to take
- all the legal and local council requirements you must comply with.

Have:
- your finances in place
- your team in place
- a full viability analysis spreadsheet
- a schedule of works that your team has approved and understands
- the foundations for a good on-going relationship with your local council officers.

If there's anything you're not clear on at this stage, or you're struggling to get hold of the right advisors or tradespeople, email us at hello@nickfox.co.uk and we'll do our best to help you.

Before you make your formal offer, go back and 'stress-test' your figures. Consult with your builder and make sure you haven't missed anything off the main budget. Even though you will be having a survey, take your builder / lead contractor around with you when you view the property for a second time. You will have spotted certain things yourself, but, assuming your builder is experienced in converting HMOs, he'll be able to advise you about potential issues, spot any problems with the fabric of the property and will probably bring up things that you might not have considered, good and bad.

When you make your offer, make sure you put it in writing and if it's below the asking price, briefly outline your reasons for settling on that value. Confirm your position, reassure them that everything's in place in terms of legals and financials, and state the suggested timescale for exchange and completion, along with any other terms you may have already discussed, such as furnishings being included. The more prepared and professional you can show yourself to be, the more likely the agent is to support you as a buyer.

Timetable, from offer to completion

The clock starts ticking from the moment your offer is accepted and the solicitors are instructed.

If you're not already familiar with the conveyancing procedure, a guide is on the next page (process and timescale may vary slightly). A standard house purchase, where a chain is involved, takes around 3 months, although you may be able to negotiate to aim for less. This is where the importance of having a good solicitor / conveyancer comes in – they can really help move the process along. But, no matter how good your legal representative is, you should still be familiar with the process, so that you know what questions to ask of both your solicitor and the agent. Again, it comes down to being informed and looking knowledgeable and professional.

Purchase	Sale
Instruct your solicitor. Compete and return their instruction paperwork - including proof of identity documents - and forward a cheque to cover their initial costs, as requested (usually c.£100).	

Estate agent sends sales particulars to all parties.

	Vendor's solicitor prepares the contract pack and sends it to your solicitor.
Contract pack is received. Your solicitor aplies for Searches, checks the Title documents and raises any enquiries with the vendor's solicitor.	
	Vendor's solicitor responds to enquiries.
Once your solicitor has received replies to enquiries, results of Searches and your mortgage offer, they will report to you on the Title and arrange for you to sign the contract. You should arrange for your deposit to be forwarded to your solicitor, in readiness for exchange.	

Both parties sign contracts.

Your solicitor confirms receipt of deposit funds.

Completion date is agreed.

Contracts are exchanged.

A completion statement is sent to you, detailing the balance required to complete (including Stamp Duty Land Tax and all other costs associated with the purchase). This must be settled with your solicitor before completion.	
Your solicitor orders mortgage funds from the lender.	
On the completion date, your solicitor transfers funds to the vendor's solicitor, pays the SDLT to HMRC and applies to the Land Registry to register you as the new owner.	
	Vendor's solicitor confirms receipt of funds and instructs the estate agent to release the keys to you.

While the purchase is going through…

Assuming you haven't been able to gain early access to the property to begin any works – which is the case most of the time, as people are usually still living there! – this is the time when you should be getting everything in order to enable you to hit the ground running as soon as you complete.

Have a good walk-through of the property

This is to enable you to complete your draft schedule of works. Your builder may already have given you all the advice you need on the second viewing, but you should have him come on this visit with you, which should take around an hour and a half. This is when you should note everything pertinent to the project, such as:

- confirming the layout & stud walls required
- details of any garage or loft conversions
- noting refits of kitchen and bathrooms
- condition of boiler
- locations of additional en-suites and other plumbing
- condition of electrics and additional sockets etc. that may be required
- number of fire doors required
- condition of décor
- parking arrangements
- general condition of fabric of property & where refurb to that will be required
- external examination

This will give you an idea of what the surveyor might report, but your builder will be able to give you an idea of costs there and then for any significant problems so you can plan any renegotiation that may be necessary. Note: It's not good practice to renegotiate the price after the sale has been agreed, but sometimes, if a significant extra cost comes to light through closer inspection, backed up by the surveyor's report, it's justified.

Confirm details with local council
Contact the relevant people you spoke to when carrying out your research, tell them that you have a purchase underway and check everything is as you understood it to be. If it turns out that something major now stands in the way – such as it being unlikely that permission for an HMO would be granted – you're still at the stage where you could pull out of the purchase, if necessary.

Firm up terms of engagement with contractors
We've worked with the same team for a long time and have a relationship where neither party feels the need for a formal, signed agreement, but for your first project with a new team, it's not a bad idea to have a 'Terms of Engagement' in writing, to include the following:

- names of both parties
- state what the job is
- confirm the timescale

- payment details (we'd recommend 40% deposit up front, stage payments and a 12% snagging retention)
- signed by both parties.

As we said earlier, one of the key elements in the success of your project is a clear line of communication with your team. Putting everything in writing ensures there won't be any debate later on about who said what. Attach it to the job quote that you've accepted from each tradesperson and file it safely.

Select fixtures, fittings and furnishings
You'll already have done your research and got quotes and prices; now's the time to firm up on everything and get it ordered. Double-check with your contractors that they're supplying everything you think they are – you don't want your plumber asking you on week three of the project when the bathroom suite's arriving, if you presumed he was ordering it!

Get your deposit funds ready
That might sound obvious, but it's amazing the number of people who forget their capital is in a savings account with restrictions on withdrawal, or who think they can give their solicitor a cheque on the day of exchange. Find out from your solicitor / conveyancer when they would like to be in receipt of the funds and make sure you allow time for electronic transfers or cheques to be cashed.

Get your works funding organised

We recommend you pay your contractors 40% up front, then make stage payments, plus there will be outlay for the fixtures, fittings and furnishings you're buying yourself, so just go back through your schedule and make sure you have money in the right places. It's worth having another conversation with your tax advisor and/ or IFA to make sure you understand the most beneficial and tax-efficient way to pay for everything.

After exchange – conversations with people

Again, we can't stress enough the importance of communication during this process, so once you have a firm completion date:

Liaise with your project manager

Confirm the team is committed to being on site from day one. Go back though your schedule of works with your project manager and make sure everything's in hand. One thing in particular he may ask you to do is book a skip, so remember to ask the question.

Apply for planning permissions, if necessary, and notify the council of when the building works will begin

We get the HMO Officer and Building Control out to the property as soon as possible after completion, so now is the time to make an appointment with them.

Contact your utility provider/s

Let them know you've exchanged, discuss the works timescale and find out what notice they need to make sure everything's live when it needs to be.

Speak to your insurer

You'll now be able to give them firm dates for work starting. Be absolutely clear on what they require you to inform them about, to make sure you're always properly covered.

Inform the neighbours

As soon as you've exchanged and have a start date for your works, let the neighbours know what's going to be happening. It's not only a matter of courtesy to warn them about potential disruption, but you also want to build good relationships with the people who will actually be your tenants' neighbours. Knock on their door to introduce yourself, so they can see you're not just another 'faceless' landlord, let them know you're happy to talk through any concerns they might have, and ask them to contact you right away if there are any problems.

DO

- Stress-test your figures before you make an offer. Do all you can at this stage to reduce the possibility of having to revise or withdraw your offer once the sale has been agreed.

- Put your offer in writing, clearly setting out your proposed terms and position.

- Make sure you understand the purchase process. That way, you can monitor how things are progressing.

- Keep referring to your schedule. The first time you do a project like this, it'll seem as though there's an enormous number of plates to keep spinning. There are a lot, but as long as you've prepared properly and got it all written down, you'll be fine!

- Keep speaking to people. Your project manager, council officers, other local property professionals...they're all here to help you. Don't be a pest, but don't be afraid to ask for advice when you need it. They'll all understand that your first project can seem quite a hurdle.

DON'T

- Forget to get your capital ready! Check with your solicitor when your deposit need to be transferred and confirm your contractors' payment schedule with your project manager.

Chapter 7

It's yours: work begins

We're repeating what we said in Chapter 2, but the tax issue is well worth bringing up again at this point. This project is, first and foremost, a financial investment and 'revenue' versus 'capital' is a division of investment and expenditure that you must be clear on before any money goes out.

Have your tax advisor give you some guidelines on how to ensure that as much of your renovation and refurbishment outgoings as possible can be allocated as revenue: that's one of the biggest tricks in terms of making this project as financially beneficial to you as it can be. Revenue items (expenditure related to operating the business of buy to let) are tax-deductible; capital items (things that improve the value of the property) can only be deducted against capital gains when you sell the property. We're not going to go into any particular detail here, and would emphasise that we're not qualified to give advice, but make sure you have this specific conversation with your advisor.

It's also a conversation you should have with your contractors, because they'll need to be very clear on their invoices with breakdowns that enable your tax advisor to prove to HMRC what's been spent where.

Now, putting HMRC to one side, let's get the renovation and refurbishment underway!

The team gets stuck in

Before you let anyone over the threshold to start work, you must ensure you have the appropriate indemnity insurance in place, to cover you for any accidents or injuries on site. Phone your insurer, explain exactly what works are about to take place and make sure you're properly protected.

The first couple of days of the project are likely to be mainly skip filling, as walls are stripped, dated fittings are ripped out and the property is cleared ready for the new works to begin.

Start off the project by having a meeting with the team just to check everyone's clear, happy and there aren't any unexpected problems. Most tradespeople on projects like this bring their own flasks and food, etc., but it's nice if you can provide some refreshments for them – electrics and water permitting! Put a kettle and some mugs on a tray, along with tea, coffee, sugar, some UHT milk and biscuits. A fed and watered team is a happy team!

Bring in the HMO Officer and Building Control

You should already have made appointments for the HMO / Amenity Standards Officer and Building Control Officer to come on site as early as possible. Go over again exactly what you're doing and if either of them raise any issues, try to resolve them there and then. This is the stage where it's not too late to change where you put stud walls and tweak any other parts of the plan.

Building Control may need to make stage visits to sign off work, so make sure you're clear on when those are required. Also ask the HMO Officer to come back when the work's almost complete, just to make sure before you send the contractors away that there's nothing else you need to do to be compliant. If the HMO Officer isn't able to help you with fire safety and a risk assessment, you should also ask the local Fire Safety Officer to visit.

Keeping on top of the schedule

As we've already said, the clearer your schedule of works, the easier it'll be to keep on top of things. With your first project, you'll probably want to spend quite a lot of time on site, so you can see how everything is done and watch the HMO coming together; just make sure you're not getting in the way!

We tend to make weekly visits and do a 'checkpoint report' for our clients every Friday, which ensures everything's on track. It details where we're up to, what's happened this week, what's happening next week and any issues that have come up. We also include pictures of the work.

It's so important to take notes and photographs all the way along. Not only is it good to have as evidence of what's happened when and the quality of work, but it'll also help you in knowing what to watch out for and what you can refine in your next project. Also, you may only be concerned with your own HMO projects right now, but you may decide a few years down the line (as we did) that you'd like to expand your business, and you'll have a well-documented portfolio of work ready to show. You may also need or want to go into a joint venture with a partner in the future – again, you'll have evidence of your project work already prepared.

Here are some photographs charting the progress of an en-suite bathroom:

www.nickfox.co.uk

And, just from a quirky aspect, we often put up pictures of the different stages of work in the hallways of our properties, as a fun and interesting talking point!

Keep an eye on the quality of work as it progresses, essentially snagging as you go along. It's much easier to put faults right as they happen, rather than waiting until the whole house is finished. Also, it helps the contractors to be clear on the standard you expect and snagging is something they expect you, as the client, to do.

If there are any big problems and you're not happy with any aspect of the work itself, the site or the tradespeople, talk to your project manager and ask him to help you resolve them. A lead builder has carpenters, plumbers, etc. that work for him, so he should be your first port of call with any concerns.

We once had a decorator whose work was just awful. He was part of our lead contractor's recommended team, so we told him we weren't happy with the quality and suggested he replace the decorator himself, or else we would have to. He agreed and found someone else whose work was much better. It's all about setting expectations, being clear on the quality you demand and trusting your instincts if you get a gut feeling something's not right. Address issues right away – don't bury your head in the sand and then complain at the end that things are wrong. As we said right at the start, you have to be good at managing people and not afraid to stand your ground if you're not happy with something or someone.

Just remember that a happy worker is a good worker, so here are our top tips for keeping your team upbeat:

1) Make sure they feel valued and appreciated. When they're doing a good job, tell them they're doing a good job.

2) Have a sense of humour – keep the atmosphere light and positive.

3) Communicate well with them. If they're not doing something as you'd like it done, tell them nicely as soon as you spot it – they should appreciate you being honest and up front.

4) Be on site. Take a real interest and show them that their work and a good atmosphere on site matters to you.

5) Be considerate. Before we visit the property, we tend to pop to the shops and arrive with sandwiches, biscuits and some drinks.

A tale of warning

If, regardless of everything we've said so far, you're tempted to cut corners and throw yourself in at the deep end, here's a case study that we hope will put you off!

Last year we sourced a property for a lady who decided she didn't want our refurbishment service and could handle it all herself. She brought in a team of eastern European builders, who didn't understand the building regulations in this country, and didn't involve either Building Control or the HMO Officer. When she asked us to go in and do an audit for her, as she lived some distance away, we actually found a couple of the builders sleeping, and what should have taken 7-8 weeks ended up taking almost twice as long.

We don't believe the work was done correctly and it certainly wasn't finished off to standard. She won't have any warranties for the work and not only runs the risk of getting a knock on the door from the local authority, but is also likely to be letting unsafe accommodation, opening her tenants up to danger and herself up to fines and prosecution if anything should go wrong in the property.

Our original research and analysis showed she should have been able to charge £500-600 per room but we later saw the property advertised at £300-£400 per room. While she thought she was saving money by not paying us, it was a complete false economy and she won't be achieving anywhere near the returns she could have.

If you're going to use a letting agent...

...or have a private property manager, bring them in early on. Let them see the property and listen to any thoughts they have on what tenants really love or hate and what things you might need to therefore tweak in your plans. If this is the person who's going to be letting your properties on your behalf, give them a reason to be enthusiastic about the home they're 'selling' to tenants and make them feel they've had a hand in creating desirable accommodation.

Marketing the rooms/property

Ideally, you want to have tenants lined up and ready to move into the property as soon as the refurbishment is finished, so you should start marketing as soon as the site is safe enough for people to walk around. (Double-check that your indemnity insurance is watertight first!). From a health & safety point of view, when taking people into the property, you must make sure you clearly state that work is currently being done and point out any particular things that might pose a danger, such as dustsheets on the floor, loose boards and electrical leads from equipment.

If this is your first project, you won't yet have any photos of what the finished property is likely to look like, but you can take external shots and have floor plan sketches and pictures of the furnishings from your suppliers, to give prospective tenants an idea. We always find that, rather than people being put off by not being able to see the end result, they're keen to secure a room in a freshly-renovated property, where everything's new.

Again, our book 'HMO PROPERTY SUCCESS' has more information about advertising and marketing so grab yourself a copy now from nickfox.co.uk or Amazon.co.uk. You can also order the audiobook from Audible.co.uk or iTunes. Kindle and iBook versions are also available.

DO

- Have another conversation with your tax advisor. Make sure you've correctly understood their advice.
- Get the council officers in asap. You don't want to have to undo work and throw your schedule out.
- Make sure your team's happy!
- Snag as you go along, and communicate with your project manager if anything's not up to standard.
- Take lots of notes and photos as work progresses.
- Begin to market the property early. You need rent to start coming in as soon as possible.

DON'T

- Cut corners. Carry out proper research, exercise due diligence and make sure you always use the right contractors, suppliers and materials for each job.
- Leave snagging to the end. It's much easier to fix problems as they arise.

Chapter 8

Fixtures, fittings and furnishings

If you're not strict with yourself, this is where you can spend way too much money for little or no gain in revenue. This is not your own home, it's a business and, while you need a good finish, you don't need the absolute highest quality.

And no matter how objective you think you are, there are a lot of people who find it hard to rein things in and stick to a strict scheme and budget when it comes to a newly acquired property. So if you find yourself tempted to push the boat out a bit, you're not alone! We actually had one client who wanted to use Farrow & Ball paint in the HMO we were refurbishing for them, because they thought the colour was nicer than the standard, hard-wearing, always-available, neutral paint we use in all our properties! That's an extreme example, but we do find that – certainly on their first project – new investors tend to want to make each property and each room within the property individual.

There's nothing wrong with the sentiment, but if you go down that road you often end up with rooms that aren't gender-neutral enough and with lots of extra accessories that tenants either disregard or damage.

Just to prove that it happens to us all, Richard will confess to having asked someone to hand-make all the curtains for his first HMO! Needless to say, he only did it that once and now gets them from Dunelm, the very reasonably-priced curtain specialist...

What tenants want

Tenants want a decent-sized bedroom that they can make their own, solid comfortable furniture, spacious communal areas and a well-equipped kitchen that's easy to keep looking clean and tidy. That's it. They're not bothered about pretty curtains, a room that's different to their neighbour's or having a wrought-iron bedstead. You can have lovely curtains made to measure for £2-3,000, or buy a similar look off the rack at a quarter of the price. As long as they close, keep the light out and the heat in, the tenant's happy – and so is your ROI.

Tenants renting rooms tend to have a 6-9 month tenure, so you're looking at an average of 3-4 changeovers every two years; that could easily be 24 different people moving through the property in that time – plus each of them has friends, bikes, boxes being lugged in and out. In short, there's quite a lot of wear and tear on an HMO. And, while it's broadly true that the more you pay, the longer something lasts, that's not what you want in an HMO. You want to be able to keep it looking fresh and know that the price you're paying for furnishings and décor is at a level where you're happy to replace items more frequently than you would ever think of doing in your own home.

That being said, don't be tempted to go for the cheapest option. Cheap flat-pack falls apart if it's moved even once and, as we've discovered, tenants often like to shift things about in their rooms. Cheap fittings, such as toilet-roll holders and kitchen taps, quickly become loose and fall apart. Your contractors, and especially the ones who you'll retain to carry out on-going maintenance, will have experience of things failing and should be able to guide you to a happy middle ground.

Develop a standard theme

The only things that really change from one HMO to another are the layout and number of rooms, and those things make absolutely no difference to the fixtures, fittings & furnishings, other than the quantity you require. So when you're selecting the 'look' for your first project, make sure you choose things that tend to be mass-manufactured and will be available for the foreseeable future. Do your shopping list properly once and it'll make life so much easier the second, third and fourth time…

There are several good reasons for using the same supplies and suppliers time and again:

- It gives you a brand and therefore a consistency of standard and appeal across all your properties, making advertising so much easier
- You can often negotiate discounts for bulk-buying
- You know you'll be able to replace an item quickly

and easily when you need to
- If your scheme is standard, it makes budgeting quicker and project managing less stressful.

We go to suppliers that are national and have a reputation for producing decent products at very reasonable prices. We're not going to go through our entire inventory here, but to give you an idea:

- We get our beds from Mr Mattress, the mattress specialist, and they're just simple divans with storage underneath - lightweight, easy to move in and out and not expensive.
- Our headboards we source from a supplier on eBay. They're just padded pieces that slide onto rails on the walls and then we push the divans up against them. They're £50 and look great.
- Wardrobes, drawers and bedside cabinets are from IKEA – flat pack, easy to put together and really solid.
- Curtains are simple ring-tops from Dunelm, the curtain specialist.
- Paint is trade Dulux or similar – easy to find in a number of outlets, meaning our maintenance team can use the same pot for touch-ups across the entire portfolio.

For carpets, you should be able to find a good local fitter who'll do an entire HMO for around £2,000, including underlay. The important thing to ensure is that it's a common product and cost-effective, i.e. hard wearing but not expensive to replace, as stained and damaged carpets are a real turn-off for tenants.

In terms of kitchen and bathroom fittings, tiles, fixtures, etc., your contractors should be able to source those for you. Bathroom suites need to be simple, white and chrome, so they look hygienic, are easy to clean and each element is easy to replace. Your kitchen should be neutral with white or chrome/silver appliances, and we find a dark grey tiled floor is hard wearing, easy to keep clean and ages well.

We referred to this earlier in the chapter, but it really is important to make the scheme gender-neutral. Keeping everything simple should mean it's equally appealing to male and female tenants.

Here are some pictures from our portfolio, so you can see the kind of finish you're looking to achieve:

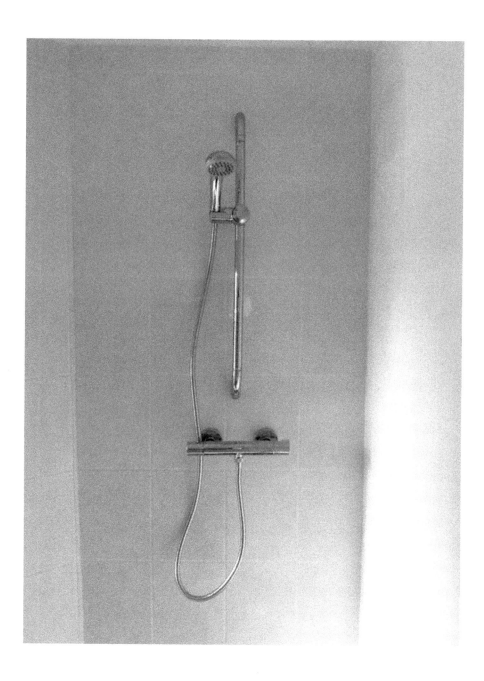

I've seen a number of properties that landlords have done to a higher spec, that are really impressive, but those tend to be in and around Central London, where people can afford to pay for and expect the very best, even in a shared house. For the vast majority of us, investing outside London, the finish we recommend is just the right balance: it looks clean, smart and modern, but (1) it's in proportion to the rent people can afford to pay, at the higher end of the scale, and (2) it fits with the ROI and monthly profit figures we look for. And those are the only two things that you need to concern yourself with.

What furniture & furnishings do I need?

We provide the following as standard in our HMOs:

Bedrooms:
- Divan bed (double or single, as required) plus headboard
- Chest of drawers
- Wardrobe
- A single bedside table
- Curtains

Kitchens:
- Double oven with 4-ring hob
- One fridge shelf and one freezer drawer per tenant – normally two fridges per property

- Washing machine
- Tumble dryer
- Microwave
- Kettle
- Vacuum cleaner
- Mop & bucket
- Clothes dryer
- Toaster

Communal area/s:
- Dining table and seating for minimum 4 people
- Curtains
- Sofa & chairs, if area permits
- Information board

Do bear in mind that if you provide lamps in bedrooms, they will have to be tested by an electrician every year, as do all other portable electrical appliances in the house (PAT). While this is easy for kitchen appliances, it may be harder to arrange access to a tenant's room and if the lamp is untested, your insurance is unlikely to cover you if it causes damage or harm to the tenant.

Keys

Over the years, we've seen and tried a number of different lock and key systems – round handles with the keyhole in the middle, auto-closing Yale locks, keypads – but by far the best, and the one we use in every property now is the master key system, also knows as 'suited' keys. Each tenant has a key that only opens the main front door and their door, while you, the maintenance team and property manager can hold a single key that accesses every room in the property. If you set up the system in the right way when you refurbish your first property, you can have a master that opens every door in every property.

It really is a great system, which you only really appreciate when you have multiple properties. Under the old system we used, where every door had its own lock and key, we had to hold a large bunch for each house. The master suited system cuts down on the time you and your maintenance team have to spend looking for keys and makes organising storage much simpler.

At £800-£900 per property, it's more expensive than having a Chubb or Yale single-key system, but it really does pay for itself time and time again. Any good master locksmith should be able to provide this for you.

DO

- Keep uppermost in your mind that this is a business. Think about your target tenant and what they want – don't be tempted to overspend for the sake of 'prettying it up'.
- Focus on a theme/scheme you can easily replicate. Source from major suppliers or local providers of good-quality basics.
- Always try to negotiate discounts for bulk buying.
- Look into getting a master suited key system.

DON'T

- Over-decorate. You'll spend more than you need to and complicate the on-going maintenance.
- Buy the cheapest option. Nine times out of ten, that's a false economy. You want cost-effective, not cheap.

Chapter 9

Tying up the project

As the renovation and refurbishment comes to an end, it's a good idea to put together a checklist to make sure you've covered everything off, in terms of the works, your legal responsibilities and making sure the property is safe, warm and ready for tenants to move in.

Snagging

Although you will have been snagging periodically throughout the project, if you don't check thoroughly that all the work has been finished off to your satisfaction and address any problems at this stage, while the contractors are still on site, things can get painful. Having to go back at a later date can cause bad feeling, delays in problems being rectified (as tradespeople are likely to be on other jobs) and potentially delay tenants moving in.

You should have agreed up front that there would be a 12% retention on the contractors' invoices until you're happy with all the work, so your team will be expecting this final snagging. Go through each room in the property, preferably with your project manager, checking that all the following is up to the standard you expect:

Bedrooms:
- Paintwork – walls, ceiling, skirting and coving all neat
- Carpet – properly fitted and finished off at edges and doorways
- Curtains – poles straight and secure at correct height
- Blinds – working properly and secure
- Light fittings – in the right place and at correct height
- Light switches – straight and operating the correct light
- Sockets – sufficient and straight
- Radiators – straight and working properly

Bathrooms:
- Paintwork – neat & correct finish
- Tiling – straight and grouting properly finished
- WC, bath, shower unit & basin – secure and edges properly sealed
- Shower & bath – work properly
- Taps, hooks & holders – secure
- Correct light fitting
- Correct ventilation
- Heated towel rail working

Kitchen:
- Paintwork – neat & correct finish
- Tiling – straight and grouting properly finished
- Flooring – solid and properly finished off at the edges

& doorways
- Units – secure & all doors and drawers functioning well
- Sink – draining properly and taps secure and working well
- Cooker & white goods - all connected and working properly
- Correct light fitting
- Correct ventilation
- Light fittings – in the right place and at correct height
- Light switches – straight and operating the correct light
- Sockets – sufficient and straight
- Radiators – straight and working properly
- Blinds – working properly and secure

Other communal areas:
- Paintwork – walls, ceiling, skirting and coving all neat
- Carpet – properly fitted and finished off at edges and doorways
- Curtains – poles straight and secure at correct height
- Blinds – working properly and secure
- Light fittings – in the right place and at correct height
- Light switches – straight and operating the correct light
- Sockets – sufficient and straight
- Radiators – straight and working properly

Make a list of any problems and have your project manager liaise with the relevant tradespeople to remedy them. Then do what will, hopefully, be a final check, confirm you're happy and have each trade issue you with a warranty for the work they've done. We expect all our contractors to give us an absolute minimum of a 6-month warranty and most are happy to guarantee their work for 12 months. Once you have those warranties, make sure you pay the contractors the balance of what you owe them as soon as possible.

Your maintenance team

Don't forget to thank your contractors and tell them how much you appreciate their hard work. You're going to need them again in the future and this is the time when you want to firm up on your on-going maintenance team. While a general handyman is the person you'll be calling on most often, you do need a plumber who is happy to come out quickly when needed, and an electrician who also won't take an age to fix problems. One of the reasons it's so important to build up a good rapport with them during the works and pay them on time is that you want them to put you to the top of the list when you need something doing.

Although you do need to keep a careful record of who holds what keys and don't want to have too many floating about, we find the easiest thing is if we give both our plumber and our electrician master keys, in addition to the handyman and cleaner. If they're good, they'll have a steady flow of work and are unlikely to be able to give you exact times when they'll be able to pop to your property between other bigger jobs. You want problems fixed quickly and if they don't have a key, it can be a real pain for your property manager – or you – to have to drop everything and rush to meet them or, worse, keep missing them so that problems drag on.

Once the contractors have finished all their work, get a cleaner in to do a thorough post-build clean (be sure to tell them that's what the job is!) to make sure the place is sparkling. And before you pay them, as with the other contractors' work, check you're happy that they've done a good job and there's no trace of building dust, etc.

Certification

In addition to guarantees and warranties for the work, you need to ensure you have the following valid certificates before you can legally let the property:

Gas Safety Certificate. This should be provided by the engineer (Gas Safe registered) who installed or serviced your boiler. It's something that needs to be done annually, so make sure both you and the engineer have diarised when it's due for renewal.

An Electrical Installation Condition Report Certificate. All fixed electrical installations must be inspected and tested by a 'Part P'-qualified electrician at least every five years. Even if your HMO falls outside licensing regulations, the local authority can still ask to see a valid certificate within seven days. So do make sure you get this from your electrician before he leaves the property.

Both these certificates should be clearly displayed in the property – we'd suggest the best place is on a nicely-fitted notice board in the kitchen.

Fire Alarm Commissioning Certificate. After the alarm system has been installed by an appropriately qualified engineer, you will be issued with this certificate, which the local council will need to see.

And, although it's not currently legally required in an HMO, where tenants are sharing facilities, make sure you file the property's **Energy Performance Certificate (EPC).** If you ever let the property as a single unit or decide to sell, you'll need it. When you bought the property, the EPC would have formed part of the documentation and it's valid for 10 years; however, if you've improved the energy efficiency, with insulation or upgrading the glazing, it's worth getting the property re-inspected to try and raise the rating.

Get your local council officers back again

This visit shouldn't throw up any issues, provided you've had the HMO Officer and Building Control out to the property previously and taken their advice, as we recommend. This time, you're just asking them to confirm that they're happy everything's been done to standard. Ask the HMO Officer to confirm in writing that the property has been registered with them and that you've complied to all amenity and fire standards. If you require one, they will issue you with a 5-year licence. The Building Control team will confirm that you've carried out all the work under a building notice and will issue you with a completion certificate.

You also need to have an appropriate person carry out your Fire Safety Risk Assessment. The HMO Officer might be able to do it for you; if not, speak to your local Fire Safety Officer or the Fire Protection Association (FPA) to make an appointment. You may have to pay somewhere in the region of £150 to £300 but that's very little for the peace of mind it offers.

Contact suppliers

You should have already spoken to your insurance and utility providers, but get back in touch with them to make sure everything's in order and you're connected and covered as you think you should be. Make sure you've registered with the council for Council Tax and that they're aware of when the property is changing from empty to occupied.

Take advertising photos before tenants move in

Although you'll be letting the rooms furnished but without linen and bedding, you should still 'dress' the rooms to take some photographs. This is where you're allowed to indulge your interior design urges! Make up the beds (you can use the same furnishings for each room that you're photographing), put some cushions and throws on them, plug in a couple of lamps and get artistic with your lens.

Similarly, put a bowl of fruit in the kitchen, a plant and towels in the bathroom, flowers on the dining table, etc. Add some colour to your neutral scheme and make the place look really inviting. And understand that it will never again look as good as it does now! If you're tempted to leave any of your dressing items, we'd recommend you don't. Vases will get broken, plants will be left to die…and so on. Remember that this is a communal house and the tenants probably won't know each other, so there's very little sense of responsibility for anything in the communal areas. As we've said before, just make sure they're clean, functional and easy to keep that way.

Make an information file for the property

A great way to welcome new tenants is with a file containing useful property information, primarily relating to health and safety. We'd suggest it contains:

- Contact details for the property manager
- Details of what to do and who to contact in an emergency
- Copies of instruction manuals for appliances

- Copies of the gas and electrical safety certificates, plus EPC
- Broadband WiFi password / connection details

Some people also include local taxi numbers, take-away menus and bus routes – it's entirely up to you. The most important contact and fire safety information should also be displayed clearly on your kitchen notice board.

And don't put any original documents in the file, as things tend to go walkabout. The best way to prepare it is to scan all the documents into an electronic file, so that you can easily print out copies if anything is missing.

Organise your own office

As we said in Chapter 1, this business demands that you're organised. Make sure you've got everything filed and noted in a way that makes sense to you. As your portfolio grows, you'll need to be able to lay your hands on the right documentation relating to the right property very easily, so take your time and make sure you're recording things properly.

A very important thing for you to keep on top of is renewal dates for certificates and licences. Many of the suppliers and service providers will contact you in good time themselves to remind you, but you need to set up some kind of alert system for:

- Annual gas safety check
- Annual PAT
- 5-yearly electrical installation check
- Annual TV licence renewal
- Annual property insurance renewal

Whoever is managing the property should also be carrying out regular fire alarm testing (we carry this out every 2 weeks) and arranging quarterly periodical room inspections.

Keep all your receipts from the refurbishment and furnishing and file them separately from the expenditure you'll have for future maintenance. We'd actually recommend you engage a bookkeeper to keep track of your income and expenditure on an on-going basis - your tax advisor will be able to point you in the direction of someone who's familiar with bookkeeping for HMO investors.

Thank the neighbours

Importantly, knock on the neighbours' doors to let them know the work is finished, thank them for their patience and understanding while the project's been going on. Let them have your or your property manager's details in case there are any problems with tenants in the future.

Be sure they understand that the property is an HMO and that there will be multiple tenants coming and going, but reassure them that the tenants will all be working adults, carefully screened, and that the HMO is permitted and approved by the council.

And that's it - you've completed your first HMO renovation and refurbishment project! If you've followed all our advice, you should now be the proud owner of a high quality, legally compliant, desirable room-rental residence that's been approved by the local authority. And as long as your research and budgeting was done properly and the project was successfully managed, you can be confident that the rental income will start coming in to give you the returns you want and deserve.

This is only the first step on the HMO journey – how you manage your buy to let business into the future will ultimately determine your success, but as long as you continue to be diligent and build relationships with the people who can help you stay on top of the game, there's no reason why you shouldn't build a profitable and enviable portfolio.

Now, on to the next project…!

Checklist

- ☐ First round of snagging completed
- ☐ HMO Officer confirmed everything's up to standard and the property has been registered with the council
- ☐ Fire Safety Risk Assessment completed
- ☐ Building Control sign-off
- ☐ Gas & electrical safety certificates obtained and displayed
- ☐ Fire Alarm Commissioning Certificate obtained and presented to council
- ☐ Warranties and guarantees for all the work obtained
- ☐ Warranties and guarantees for all appliances registered
- ☐ Second snagging completed to satisfaction
- ☐ Balance of snagging retainer (12%) paid to contractor
- ☐ Full commercial clean of property
- ☐ Rooms dressed and photographs taken
- ☐ Neighbours thanked
- ☐ Correct number of keys in hand
- ☐ Cleaner engaged for on-going cleaning of communal areas & key given
- ☐ Handyman (or similar) engaged for maintenance & key given
- ☐ Plumber and electrician given keys

☐ Gardener engaged

☐ Council tax, TV licence and utilities all in order

☐ Information file left in the property

☐ Administration procedures set up

PART THREE:

ONWARDS AND UPWARDS!

Ready to apply what you've learned?

Great! Here's even more from Nick Fox Property Mentoring

Thanks for taking the time to read this book - hopefully you've found it helpful and are inspired to put some or all of it into practice!

If you'd like to extend your knowledge, the next step is to check out our website, where you'll find lots of free information and details of our mentoring packages.

We offer a range of options to suit all needs, from short intensive taster sessions to more comprehensive packages that will give you a deeper understanding of property investment and the buy to let market, focusing on the rewards and implications of building an HMO portfolio:

- Half-day 'HMO Education and Tour'
- One-day 'Intensive HMO Property Mentoring Course'
- Two-day 'Intensive HMO Property Mentoring Course'
- 12 months' full access to and support from Nick Fox and his Power Team

Whichever package you choose, you can be assured that Nick's commitment to your personal property goals are absolute. Nick and his team get a real kick out of watching others grow their property portfolios by helping them implement the most successful methods that have been tried and tested over many years.

As skilled and experienced professionals, we present our mentoring sessions in such a way that they're easy to understand, while enabling highly effective learning. The acute insights and practical methodology on offer will help you to take your property business to the next level and secure financial independence for you and your loved ones.

Check out our website **nickfox.co.uk** or call us on **01908 930369** to find out more.

Find us on
FACEBOOK Nick Fox Mentor
TWITTER NickFoxPropertyMentoring
EMAIL hello@nickfox.co.uk
TEL 01908 930369

NICK FOX PROPERTY MENTORING
Suite 150, MK Business Centre, Foxhunter Drive,
Linford Wood, Milton Keynes MK14 6BL

Write a review and get free stuff!

If you've enjoyed what you've read, why not tell other people and bag yourself some free stuff in the process?

Simply write a review of this book – or any of the other books in the 'SUCCESS' series – and publicise it via:

- Amazon
- iTunes
- Facebook
- Twitter
- A blog

… or any other online or offline publication.

Then email an image or link to us at hello@nickfox.co.uk.

We'll thank you via Twitter and you'll get back some exclusive property investment tools or samples of our latest materials to help you stay focused and up to date in your investment journey.

Thanks in advance and we hope to hear from you soon!

Amazon reviews for...

HMO Property Success

'A brilliant book'
What sets Nick Fox' book apart from others is the amount of practical detail and advice. It provides a solid and clean framework and a step-by-step guide on how to find, fund, fill and run a profitable house in multiple occupancy. This book has no fluff – it is a very valuable and easy read.
nc3134, 17 Nov 2013

'A MUST read for any HMO owner or investor'
This book is concise, well written, well informed and very practical. I have many other property books but this is by far the best and a must for anyone wanting to invest in HMO property.
Mark MTC, 23 Jan 2014

'Best Property Investment Book'
This no-nonsense approach will guide anyone who is interested in the HMO market into a successful investment; unlike many other publications that purport to be able to help people "get rich quick" with "no money down"; this insightful guide is

realistic and proven.
RegSupport, 17 Nov 2013

'Step by step guide to HMO investing'
It is rare in a property book of this kind to find so much solid advice and what must have been hard-earned knowledge - in comparison most other books on the subject provide next to no real information on how to get started. Everyone thinking of getting into hmo property investing should buy this book!
AndyP, 1 Dec 2013

'Great book – especially for those looking to start building a HMO portfolio'
I'm not new to property but am about to start building a HMO portfolio and this book gave me some excellent advice not available in other publications. It also gave me the confidence to proceed down the HMO route!
Stephen Whall, 28 March 2014

Using an easy to understand and simple format, this book is highly effective and informative, neither superficial nor "salesy". A pleasant read for anyone who is time poor and wants to learn HMO property investing.
K Devos, 9 Jan 2014

'Excellent Book'
There are no hard sells, no 'get rich quick' advice, it simply tells

you that Nick's investment strategy has proven to give successful results. I strongly advise you to read this book if you are serious about investing.

Elda Breuer, 5 Feb 2014

The Secrets of Buy to Let Success

'Another great book by Nick Fox!'
Having read HMO Property Success, I had high expectations and was very impressed by how this book delivered. It is written clearly and concisely to provide intuitive and straightforward examples that anyone can relate to. There are no empty promises on making lots of profit with no investment. Nick's book simply explains how property can make you financially independent and what you need to have in order to have the best chance to be successful. This book will help me make better, more informed decisions about my long-term plan.
nc3134, 3 Feb 2015

'Great book with loads of useful information'
As a buy to let landlord myself, I like books that have lots of details in them. After reading tons of books in this field and also attending numerous seminars, I feel this is the best collection of information I've seen in a long while.
MarkMTC, 24 Jan 2015

'A practical, no-nonsense guide to property investing'
As opposed to some material on the market that suggests property is a no-risk, no-investment, high-return vehicle, Nick Fox's book offers a

clear, realistic view of what it takes to be successful. As a new property investor, I was looking for a book that I could relate to, feel comfortable with. Nick's book offered just that - scenarios and field-based examples that made me, a novice, feel confident, bold and capable. Whether buying through an auction or opening an HMO, I was able to find handy advice in this book. Most importantly, Nick has clearly and diligently highlighted the risks of every undertaking so there were no surprises along the way. This book is a breath of fresh air...

NJC 001, 1 April 2015

'One of the best books I have seen in the market on this topic'
I was looking for a book that walks me through each step of acquiring and running a buy to let property. I have to admit this is one of the best books I have seen in the market on this topic. Each chapter explains each phase of the process and gives practical hits and tips. A 'must read' book for anyone looking to buy a buy-to-let property!
Sanjay, 7 April 2015

'Simple, yet detailed'
Having read his other book, 'HMO Property Success', I thought it worthwhile to follow it up with this one. Yet again he has DELIVERED! Not only has he managed to keep it reader-friendly, but there is tones of brilliant advice to be taken.
Gabes, 6 April 2015

Property Investment Success

'A great resource for property investors'

An excellent tool for any new or seasoned Property Investor / Landlord.

A well-structured, informative book offering the tools to get organised in the property investment world. I have read a few titles from this author and find his style of writing very easy to digest. If you have any doubts about your current pension scheme then I would recommend you take the time to read a book like this, no get rich quick schemes here, just an extremely practical look into property investment, and in my eyes a must read!

MarkMTC, 24 Jan 2015

'Easy to read and credible'

This book has influenced my outlook of the future. I've never been convinced by pensions, somebody else having control of my money for decades until my retirement age... Nick's book showed me that there is an alternative, that it is possible to take control. He helped me understand how hard work, discipline and determination can pay off through property investment so you can build a future on your own terms. This book is an eye-opener and a fantastic value for money.

NJC 001, 1st April 2015

'Great job explaining investment strategies'

When I started my property investment journey, I struggled to find a single book that explains that various investment strategies (cash flow, capital growth, etc.) in one place. Because of this, I spent a great deal of time and money attending various seminars and courses to gain this knowledge. This book does a great job explaining all these strategies in one place, making it essential reading for anyone embarking on a property investment journey.
Sanjay, 7 April 2015

Even more...

...from Nick Fox Property Mentoring.

Thank you for taking the time to read our book; we hope you've found it helpful. If you'd like to extend your knowledge, please check out our website, where you'll find a wealth of free information and details of our mentoring packages.

We offer a range of mentoring options to suit all needs, from short intensive taster sessions to more comprehensive packages that will give you a deeper understanding of property investment and the buy to let market, focusing on the rewards and implications of building an HMO portfolio.

Various choices available include:

- Half-day 'HMO Education and Tour'
- One-day 'Intensive HMO Property Mentoring Course'
- Two-day 'Intensive HMO Property Mentoring Course'
- 12 months' full access to and support from Nick Fox and his Power Team

Whichever package you choose, you can be assured that Nick's commitment to your personal property goals are absolute. Nick and his team get a real kick out of watching others grow their property portfolios by helping them implement the most successful methods that have been tried and tested over many years.

As skilled and experienced professionals, we present our mentoring sessions in such a way that they are easy to understand, while enabling highly effective learning. The acute insights and practical methodology on offer will help you to take your property business to the next level and secure financial independence for you and your loved ones.

Check out our website **www.nickfox.co.uk** or call us on **01908 930369** to find out more.

Find us on FACEBOOK Nick Fox Mentor TWITTER @foxytowers
www.nickfox.co.uk EMAIL hello@nickfox.co.uk TEL 01908 930369
NICK FOX PROPERTY MENTORING
14 Wharfside Bletchley Milton Keynes MK2 2AZ

Read on...

Collect the set of books by Nick Fox to help you achieve financial freedom through property investment.

HMO PROPERTY SUCCESS

Do you want a secure financial future that starts sooner, rather than later as you're approaching retirement? By investing in multi-let properties, you can double or even triple the level of rental income generated by single letting, and realise positive cash flow from the start. In this book, multiple business owner and investor, Nick Fox, clearly guides you through the steps to building an HMO portfolio that delivers both on-going income and a tangible pension or lifestyle pot.

ISBN: 978-0-9576516-0-9
RRP: £9.99

PROPERTY INVESTMENT SUCCESS

How does your financial future look?
If you haven't reviewed your pension provision for a while or aren't completely happy with how your current investments are performing, you should take a closer look at property. In this book, Nick Fox discusses the pros and cons of traditional pensions and makes the case for property as a robust alternative investment vehicle.
He looks at how property can deliver different kinds of returns at different times and shows how you can build a tailored portfolio that perfectly satisfies your own future financial needs.

ISBN: 978-0-9576516-4-7
RRP: £9.99

THE SECRETS OF BUY TO LET SUCCESS

Are you looking for a sound investment that can give you both income and growth on your capital, but nervous about the future of the property market? This book will put your mind at rest. In The Secrets of Buy to Let Success, Nick Fox shares his knowledge and expertise about the market, guiding the reader step by step through the basics of building a solid and profitable property business - even through an economic crisis. If you're completely new to property investment, this book is a great place to start.

ISBN: 978-0-9927817-2-9
RRP: £9.99

101 TOP TIPS FOR PROPERT INVESTMENT SUCCESS

Whether you're looking to focus purely on HMOs, build a varied portfolio of rental properties, or employ a number of different strategies to make money from property, '101 TOP TIPS' is full of useful information that will help keep you at the top of the property investment business.

Nick Fox has spent the past decade amassing a highly profitable buy to let portfolio and continues to invest in a variety of property projects and business ventures. His tailored mentoring programmes have helped many aspiring investors realise their own potential in the property field.

ISBN: 978-0-9935074-9-6 | RRP: £9.99

FIRST TIME PROPERTY DEVELOPER

Interested in developing property for profit ? Don't know where to start? Let experienced property expert, Nick Fox, lead you through the process. Nick will show you how to find the property, add genuine value to it by developing and refurbishing and then explain how to sell on for profit or rent out for income.

ISBN: 978-0-9576516-4-7
RRP: £9.99

COMPLETE PROPERTY INVESTMENT SUCCESS

This indispensable trilogy takes you through the pros and cons of property as an investment vehicle, looks at the business of buy to let and the different ways you can make money from property, then goes into detail about how to successfully source, refurbish and let out highly cash-positive houses in multiple occupation.

ISBN: 978-0-9927817-0-5
RRP: £26.99

COMPLETE HMO PROPERTY SUCCESS

This HMO 'superbook' is essential reading for anyone who's starting out in property investment and wants to generate income.

It begins by looking at investing in Houses in Multiple Occupation as a business and takes you through how to successfully source, refurbish, let out and manage a highly cash-positive portfolio.

The second part then focuses on the all-important renovation stage. It details how to budget, plan your works, manage your project and carry out the refurbishment in such a way that your HMO performs as you need it to and you get the returns you're looking for.

A prolific and highly successful investor, Nick's personal portfolio extends to more than 200 properties, both shared accommodation and single household lets – and he also has interests in several development projects around the UK.

ISBN: 978-0-9935074-0-3 I RRP: £19.99

Available now online at
www.amazon.co.uk & www.nickfox.co.uk
Books, iBook, Kindle & Audio

Find us on FACEBOOK Nick Fox Mentor TWITTER NickFoxPropertyMentoring
www.nickfox.co.uk EMAIL hello@nickfox.co.uk TEL 01908 930369
NICK FOX PROPERTY MENTORING
14 Wharfside Bletchley Milton Keynes MK2 2AZ

Testimonials

For Nick...

"I met Nick a number of years ago and was immediately struck by his deep knowledge and experience in the field of property investing. No problem is ever too great a challenge for Nick - his creative entrepreneur spirit is a joy to behold. He is both dynamic and detailed, great fun to work with and quite truly inspirational. He is now my business partner and good friend."
Richard Leonard

"Nick and his team are the real deal. Their knowledge and help in moving my investment project forward has been invaluable. Without their expertise I would not have been able to reach my personal property goals or milestones."
Richard Felton, UK

"Great book, great guy and great results for me after I read 'HMO Property Success'. I've now replaced my job with passive income from HMO properties. Thanks, Nick!"
C.Clark, Bedford

"Nick has clearly got a huge amount of knowledge in his field, and having his support and experience has given me the increased confidence to make my first steps into investing."
Craig Smith, Edinburgh

"Nick is a very experienced property professional. His practical advice on setting goals, the pros and cons of this type of investment and how to minimise risks and properly manage a growing portfolio are essential in what can be a very complex investment. Nick's mentoring is not a get-rich-quick formula but a clear and concise way of demonstrating how a solid property investment strategy can be put into action. And the results are well worth it."
D.Wright, Aberdeen

"I have spent money in the past on various property courses, where you are taught in a group in a classroom, and those have not really helped me. This one-to-one mentoring with Nick was brilliant, as I was actually seeing his business and properties, meeting tenants, getting lots of advice and seeing what worked well and what didn't in a live situation. I have booked another two days with Nick in my home city next week, to look at various properties and hopefully start my journey as a full-time property investor, and I cannot wait! I highly recommend this type of mentoring!"
James Robinson, Hull

"Both Sarah and I cannot express how much help Nick has been to our property business over the last two years. His support and

knowledge have been invaluable. We would thoroughly recommend his mentoring to any budding investor."
Stuart Lewis, Northampton

"Thank you so much for your patience, professionalism and general understanding during our three-day mentoring programme. The visit to see how your office and HMO business runs was incredible and so, so helpful. Without it we would have been at a complete loss. With your guidance and help we have now purchased our first HMO property and look forward to keeping in touch to show you our profitable progress!"
Rebecca Santay-Jones, Harrow

"I first met Nick in the autumn of 2012 when I was looking for someone to guide me through my first HMO purchase. Nick's mentoring was invaluable and gave me such a good grounding - not just in HMOs, but in how to run a successful property business - that I have been able to move forward with real confidence as my business has grown. Even now, if there is something I am uncertain of, or I just want to bounce an idea around, I'm very grateful to have Nick in my corner. He has such wide-ranging experience in the industry and I value his opinion greatly. The income my portfolio already provides gives me the option of going part-time in my day job and in the coming months, as I grow the business further, I fully intend to become a full-time property investor and landlord."
Andy Potter, Fareham

For Richard…

"Over the last 10 years I have met and worked with some of the finest companies and people in property. None of them outshine Richard Leonard. His warm, sincere and honest delivery of his vast property knowledge is a breath of fresh air and his playful sense of humour engages with his audience every time. Richard's project management skills are industry leading, as is his attention to detail with every client and project."
Nick Fox

"Richard successfully combines laser-focused project management skills and a pragmatic insight to support his property clients in their HMO journey to wealth."
Jarrad Murray CA PMP, worked with Richard in Blue Chip Corporates

"Richard has been passionate about property for the twenty plus years I have known him. By working strategically to develop his portfolio he has been able to turn that passion into sustainable income and this is an excellent opportunity to learn from his hard-won expertise."
Nicola Turner, Barnet

"I wish I'd met Richard a lot sooner during my career as a property investor. He's a real pro who demonstrates success with good planning and great action. His expertise continually grows and he's the bloke you can trust to help you on your way when it

comes to HMOs, whether he's teaching you how it's done, sourcing suitable properties for you or taking care of the whole package."
Judith Morgan, Business Mentor

"I have the pleasure of working with Richard to fill his HMOs with lovely tenants after their refurbishments. We regularly get great feedback on the quality of the rooms. A great person to work with who is infectiously positive and passionate about sharing his knowledge and experience to help others."
K. Appleby, Lettings Manager, Stevenage Lettings Ltd.

"He is the most innovative, professional and caring person I've ever met - you can totally rely on Rich!"
Martin Roche, mentee and professional partner

"I've known Richard for a number of years, helping him to source investment opportunities. He's the go-to guy for HMOs."
Jack Draper, Estate Agent, Stevenage

"I have worked with Richard for a few years now and wish that all my clients were as knowledgeable and pleasant to deal with. Richard is very thorough and well organised."
Julia Harling, Property Solicitor

"Mr Delivery, Mr Quality, Mr Empathy - just a few of the qualities you'll find he embodies when you're working or dealing with Richard!"
Edward Clark, Business Associate